SALVATORE BABON

M000310998

SIXTEEN FOR '16

A Progressive Agenda for a Better America

320.473   5-15

POLICY PRESS **SHORTS** INSIGHTS

First published in Great Britain in 2015 by

Policy Press
University of Bristol
1-9 Old Park Hill
Bristol
BS2 8BB
UK
t: +44 (0)117 954 5940
pp-info@bristol.ac.uk
www.policypress.co.uk

North America office:
Policy Press
c/o The University of Chicago Press
1427 East 60th Street
Chicago, IL 60637, USA
t: +1 773 702 7700
f: +1 773 702 9756
sales@press.uchicago.edu
www.press.uchicago.edu

© Policy Press 2015

British Library Cataloguing in Publication Data
A catalogue record for this book is available from the British Library.

Library of Congress Cataloging-in-Publication Data
A catalog record for this book has been requested.

ISBN 978-1-4473-2440-9 (paperback)
ISBN 978-1-4473-2442-3 (ePub)
ISBN 978-1-4473-2443-0 (Mobi)

The rights of Salvatore Babones to be identified as the author of this work has been
asserted by him in accordance with the Copyright, Designs and Patents Act 1988.

All rights reserved: no part of this publication may be reproduced, stored in a
retrieval system, or transmitted in any form or by any means, electronic, mechanical,
photocopying, recording, or otherwise without the prior permission of Policy Press.

The statements and opinions contained within this publication are solely those of the
author and not of the University of Bristol or Policy Press. The University of Bristol
and Policy Press disclaim responsibility for any injury to persons or property resulting
from any material published in this publication.

Policy Press works to counter discrimination on grounds of gender, race,
disability, age and sexuality.

Cover design by Andrew Corbett
Front cover: image kindly supplied by Getty
Printed and bound in Great Britain by CMP, Poole
The Policy Press uses environmentally responsible print partners

"Yet another progressive agenda, you might well say. But this one is different. It is so sensible and straightforward that it actually dispels the cloudy and complicated debates that confuse us about our policy options."
Frances Fox Piven, Professor of Political Science and Sociology, City University of New York

"Salvatore Babones' new book provides useful insights on many of the most important issues facing the country. The political picture will be far brighter if his list of priorities were at the top of the national agenda."
Dean Baker, Co-director, Center for Economic and Policy Research, Washington DC

"This book brilliantly critiques and offers concrete practices and policy suggestions about how to move from calls for empty reform to real change. A must-read."
Professor Henry A. Giroux, McMaster University Chair for Scholarship in the Public Interest

"Reminds us of those times when Democrats, Republicans, Socialists, Green Party activists and Independents could all be proud of America and proposes how we can relaunch a common vision for the future."
Judith Blau, Professor Emerita, University of North Carolina

This book is dedicated with
gratitude to Leslie Thatcher

Contents

Preface

American politics are on the wrong track, and everybody knows it. The federal government is mired in perpetual budget paralysis. Congressional approval ratings are the stuff of comedy punch lines. Fox News is also a 24-hour-a-day joke that just happens not to be very funny. Politicians are very careful never to say anything in public; saying something can only get you in trouble. And policies that could shape the life chances of millions of Americans for generations to come are formulated on the basis of focus group testing of three-second sound-bites. That is sheer madness. We can and should do better.

I am not a politician, a political activist, or a policy analyst. The last time I held political office it was as Imperator of my high school Latin club. I rarely sign petitions and to my shame I have never walked in a protest march. It should go without saying that I have never been shocked with a TASER™ electroshock device, pepper sprayed, arrested, or imprisoned for expressing my beliefs. I know people who have, and I look up to them as heroes in the fight for justice. I am not a hero.

I am a professional sociologist and social statistician. My other books have titles like *Methods for Quantitative Macro-Comparative Research* and *Latent Variables and Factor Analysis*. This book is different, because things have become so bad that I felt an obligation to do something to help make them better. The United States is making a mess of its social, economic, and political policies. With an election coming up in 2016—a Presidential election that is wide-open for candidates from both major parties—I felt it was important that social science have a say. The country should be moving forward, not backward, and social science has the potential to help guide progress toward a better and brighter future.

As my family and friends know all too well, at the personal level I am one of the most conservative people on the planet. I was born on October 5, 1969, and for the most part I haven't changed since. I grew up in a highly commercialized but relatively benign corporate America. The greatest influences on my moral development were *Super Friends* and *Schoolhouse Rock*, children's programs on the ABC television network. I went on to win a 1984 high school civics competition (and astonished a crowd of administrators, teachers, and fellow students) by reciting the six purposes stated in the Preamble to the Constitution from memory. Thirty years later I understand from Wikipedia that I owe that victory to *Schoolhouse Rock* singer-songwriter Lynn Ahrens. To Lynn a big, belated "thank you." To ABC television ... well, I guess it's for the best.

I was born smack in the middle of Generation X to pre-Baby Boom parents and was thus educated mainly by young, idealistic Baby Boom teachers. Unknown to me at the time, the movies, music, and other pop culture I loved were almost all produced by Baby Boomers. Like many other Gen Xers I took the morals espoused by these (slightly) older idealists at face value. We did as they said, not as they did. The actual children of the Baby Boomers, today's Millennials, may occupy the public streets and squares protesting perceived injustices. All credit to them for doing so. But we weren't brought up like that. We were brought up in the quiet confidence that America was fantastic and getting better every year—that progress was not only desirable but inevitable.

That firm belief is the reason we became so disillusioned when we found that progress had simply stopped around the time we were born. Many of us were bewildered by this fact, if not in shock. As a sociologist, I found it simply incredible. In the first decade of the 2000s the main focus of my academic research was income distribution. My research involved the statistical analysis of data from more than a hundred countries. When looking at the distribution of income in the United States, I was amazed to find that after adjusting for inflation most jobs paid the same in the 2000s as they had in the 1970s. I was by no means the first person to discover this. But in my thirties it was a new discovery for me, and I couldn't believe my computer screen.

At the time I was at the University of Pittsburgh teaching a one-semester global sociology class. I took the pedagogical approach of putting US data in a global context. I compared the US to other countries, both as a yardstick to help students understand the other countries of the world and as a way to teach them about the United States itself. Most other developed countries have some form of universal health insurance, universally affordable college education, unemployment benefits people can actually live on, strong environmental regulation, and many of the other good things that come in the wake of civilization.

At the end of my last lecture in April 2008, one of my students came up to me and asked if I had ever considered moving overseas. I told her I was leaving the following week, and six and a half years later I am still living in Sydney, Australia. Much to the chagrin of many of my colleagues at the University of Sydney I am still very much an American, and proud of it. And I am still a very conservative person. I work hard and I don't play very much. I'm probably not much fun to be around. My political convictions consist mainly of a commitment to democratic processes and a desire for rational social policy. If I am a leftist, it is only because the center has moved so far to the right. In the spirit of Barry Goldwater, I am certain that it is the country that has changed, not me. I sincerely hope that it will change back soon.

I won't bore everyone with an Academy Awards list of "thank yous". Suffice it to say that I really do appreciate all the help I've received from everyone who has been associated with this work, including especially my friends at Truthout and at Policy Press. I do, however, feel obliged to thank six people specifically by name.

First, obviously, and for all the usual reasons. I have to thank my ever-supportive wife, Aija Bruvere. Equally obviously, I must thank John Cavanagh, Director of the Institute for Policy Studies, for his generosity in contributing a foreword to this work and in making me feel welcome as a member of the IPS community. I would like to thank my editor at IPS, Emily Schwartz Greco, for patiently teaching me some of the basics of writing for a general, non-academic audience. I would like to thank my other editor at IPS, Sam Pizzigati, for "discovering" me and bringing me into the IPS community. I would like to thank Alison Shaw, Director of the Policy Press and my editor there, for her constant encouragement and for her unwavering faith in me and in this book. And finally I would like to thank my editor at Truthout, Leslie Thatcher, to whom this book is dedicated.

A final note: all author's royalties generated by this book will be donated directly to the not-for-profit news organization Truthout. The book's publishers, Policy Press and the University of Chicago Press, are both not-for-profit organizations that genuinely work in the public interest. When all is said and done, a lot of people are not profiting when you buy this book! On their behalf, thank you for buying the book; and on my behalf, thank you for reading it.

Salvatore Babones
Sydney, Australia
October 5, 2014

Foreword

Progressives, inebriated by hope for the "change we can believe in," were a key force in electing Barack Obama by a relative landslide in 2008. But then most of us promptly forgot how change happens in this country.

Up through the 1970s, progressives could take on big corporate interests and win by having good ideas and pressing them forcefully. Take, for example, the Fair Labor Standards Act 1938 and the Clean Air Act 1963. However, by the late 1970s, large corporations began to understand that for relatively modest investments in lobbyists, they could corrupt the American political system.

Over these past 35 years, aided by Supreme Court decisions, corporations have rigged the rules in their favor. When President Obama took office, these forces were poised to thwart or water down many of the ideas that propelled him into the White House. Progressives, on the other hand, underestimated the need to keep up the heat on Obama and Congress to carry out their election mandate. Three weeks into office, Obama did pass an economic stimulus bill that helped put many people back to work, even if it did little to position our economy for a cleaner future less dependent on fossil fuels. Obama has also presided over a major cultural shift around gay rights.

But otherwise, the wins have been thin. On big issues like healthcare and Wall Street reform, we won only a fraction of the agenda we wanted. Given the enormous power of corporations over our political system, progressives still would have faced high hurdles even if they had put more into "street heat" pressure on policymakers. But we could have won much more, particularly in 2009 and 2010 when Democrats controlled the House, Senate, and White House. Six years of disappointment in Obama and six years of widespread revulsion of the corporate takeover of our politics has left many progressives demoralized. It's not that people have abandoned their progressive values. For example, polls show that a large majority of Americans support raising the minimum wage, believe the gap between CEO and worker pay is far too wide, support action to combat global warming, and want to tax Wall Street transactions.

But people are reluctant to think big, for fear of getting their hopes dashed once again. Ideas are shrinking. Into this relative void steps Salvatore Babones. One of the world's leading experts on inequality, he is also a broad-based thinker who offers in these pages a bold, comprehensive agenda for progressive change. His 16 policy areas are not a laundry list, but rather an interrelated set of goals that would go a long way towards transforming our country from one captured by narrow corporate interests to one that is more sustainable, fair, and peaceful.

These are ideas you can get excited about, and they have the verve to capture the progressive energy that abounds in this country and steer it towards the right targets.

John Cavanagh
Director, Institute for Policy Studies
Washington
September, 2014

INTRODUCTION

Change is random; progress moves in one direction. Every generation in American politics debates a set of core principles that once agreed are agreed for all time. Free speech was guaranteed in the 18th century. Slavery was outlawed in the 19th century. Women got the vote in the 20th century. None of these core principles will ever be revisited. They are taken for granted by all politicians, left and right.

This book suggests 16 core policies that together form a progressive political agenda for the 21st century. These 16 policies should be on every progressive's list for the 2016 US elections (and beyond) because they reflect principles that no reasonable person of the future will question. Many of the positions taken in this book may appear ambitious or even utopian today, but when our grandchildren look back from the 22nd century they will seem as obvious as free speech, the end of slavery, and votes for women.

The book is thus designed as a kind of progressive field manual for the 2016 US elections. It presents only straightforward and easy-to-understand social policies that are fully consistent with well-established social science. The arguments for these policies are presented in a jargon-free way and are illustrated using official US government data and other standard sources. Since none of the policies presented in the book are scientifically contentious, academic sources are cited sparingly. The focus is on exposition rather than argumentation.

For example, no one in academic social science seriously doubts that our children should be educated by public schools, not educated by for-profit firms. Calls for school privatization, greater standardized testing, and the destruction of teachers' unions come overwhelmingly from privately funded think tanks and business schools, not from social science academics. Thus Chapter 3 on public education takes for granted the academic consensus in favor of well-funded public schools that involve multiple stakeholders in the broad-spectrum education of our children.

Academically contentious questions in public education—the choice of curriculum, optimum teaching methods, the benefits of diversity, gender differences in learning, methods for addressing social disadvantage, etc.—are entirely absent. The exclusion of these highly contentious issues makes it possible for the chapter to address the "big issues" in public education in a brief essay of 2,000 words. While many elements in society would vehemently disagree with the views expressed in this chapter, very few social scientists would find much to quibble with.

Similarly with the other 15 chapters. All progressives could name many policies that they would want to see included in this book that aren't, but few could find fault with the 16 policies that are. Highly contentious issues involving unsettled social science or genuinely legitimate differences of opinion have intentionally been left off the list. Immigration reform? Too difficult. Care for child refugees? No problem. There are many important things we should be doing as a country that aren't mentioned in this book. This book is meant to be a starting point for the progressive movement, not a final destination.

Also in an effort to focus the book on 16 top must-have policies for the 2016 election many no-brainer progressive policies have been left off the list. Some of them, like civil rights for sexual minorities (including gay marriage), have been left off because they are already happening and almost certain to move forward no matter who wins the election. Others, like promoting racial equality, are millennial challenges for all of society that cannot be solved by specific government action. Still others, like national gun control, would be difficult to implement without Constitutional change. And many, many more have been excluded just to keep the list manageable.

And that's the whole point: the 16 progressive policies presented here are manageable. They can be accomplished by an ambitious President with a solid majority in Congress. They are all potentially or actually very popular, meaning that a Presidential candidate could leverage the power of the people to push them through even the most recalcitrant Congress. A future President who put these 16 policies one by one on the national agenda and made a strong argument in favor of each would make history while making the country and the world a better place for generations to come.

For the benefit of future Presidents who want to make history (and for the thousands of campaigners and support personnel who will support them) the 16 chapters of this book are supported by extensive citations to data sources, articles, and reports of all kinds. A quick glance to the Notes section at the end of the book will reveal 267 endnotes, or an average of about one note for every 120 words of text. These have not been included merely to make the book look more scholarly. In fact, most of the notes are not scholarly at all.

The notes are there to help interested readers follow up on the issues raised in the text in the most effective possible ways. They have been carefully curated to link to the most comprehensive and useful sources of information on any given topic. Where possible, data have been traced back to their original sources instead of being culled from press reports and online echo chambers. Where press reports have been used, every effort has been made to select the most informative among many available reports. And nearly all of the materials cited in the notes are available online.

So much careful attention has been paid to the notes that an appropriate subtitle for this book might have been "a progressive guide to the internet." Since that is the case, some might wonder why web addresses have not been provided. The simple fact is that web addresses are constantly changing; most of the links in most of the sources cited in the notes no longer work. Instead of web addresses the notes provide all the information necessary for finding sources using a search engine: author, title, organization, date. A simple search using the information in any of the notes should quickly yield the desired document.

Dozens of important national and international organizations appear in the notes. One does not: the American Legislative Exchange Council (ALEC). For those who don't know about ALEC, it is a shadowy organization that helps state legislators network with corporate lobbyists to craft uniform legislation that can be taken back to state capitols around the country for surreptitious passage below the radar of the national media. It works to implement in all 50 states policies that could never pass muster in the United States. It is a kind of conservative legion of doom that looms behind every evil plot to undermine American freedom and social democracy.

Just as ALEC flies below the radar screen of the mainstream media it flew below the radar screen of this book. This is a book about national policies for the United States, not a book about 50 state policies for a divided America. Judged on the content of the 16 chapters of this book ALEC would almost certainly go sixteen for 16 in the wrong direction, and then some. Suffice it to say that this is not a book about

ALEC. That book has yet to be written; surely someone is already writing it. Godspeed.

Leaving aside this legislative legion of doom, if the American people have one major flaw it is that they are too open-minded. You can fool all the people part of the time—and stop right there. That's the problem. The right-wing alternatives to all of the policies proposed in this book have been presented to the public (mostly by rich people or business-funded think tanks) as fresh, original, even breakthrough thinking. They are "wouldn't it be great if ..." and "perhaps the time has come to consider ..." types of ideas. And they are wrong.

On TV and in the movies whenever hero's scientist friend says of a desperate gambit that "it just might work" it almost always does. In real life it almost always doesn't. In real life, crazy ideas that promise something for nothing ("cutting taxes on the rich will generate increased tax revenue") are just that: crazy ideas. Most Americans have no trouble spotting a crazy investment scam or get-rich-quick scheme. Somehow we are more much more credulous, gullible even, when it comes to our country.

Our country doesn't need any more crazy conservative schemes that promise to fix problems by ignoring them, outsourcing them, or relying on the "magic of the market" to solve them. What the country needs is sound government based on established social science, underpinned by a basic sense of human decency. What the country needs is progress, and progress takes hard work, good judgment, and at least a little sacrifice. You don't get something for nothing. But if everyone makes small but strategic sacrifices for the common good, everyone can get much more back in return.

That's called investment, and investment in the future is what progress is all about. The whole point of the progressive movement is that progress is never achieved; progress always progresses. This book sets out 16 policy goals for 2016. If by some miracle we achieve them, we should set another twenty for 2020. Even if we don't achieve them, we should set another twenty for 2020. But for now, 16 will do. I challenge any American to look in the mirror and ask: If we really adopted all 16 of the policies laid out in this book, would America be a better place? If the answer is yes, let's set a goal to get them adopted. And let's call on every 2016 Presidential candidate to lead us toward that goal.

1
CREATE JOBS

In January 2008 the US economy provided full-time employment for 122 million people and part-time employment for another 24 million. Then the recession hit, followed by the recovery. The end result was that by January 2014 the US economy had lost more than three million full-time jobs and replaced them with just over two million part-time jobs.[1] At the end of this five-year period there were one million fewer Americans with any kind of employment than at the beginning, and many more Americans who were stuck with only part-time work. Over that same five-year period, the US adult population grew by more than 14 million.[2] In ordinary times about 65% of the US adult population actively participates in the labor force.[3] The fact that in 2014 there were 14 million more adults than in 2008 means that in ordinary times the US economy would need about 9 million more jobs to accommodate them. No matter how you add up the figures, the jobs just aren't there.

Officially, the economic recession associated with the global financial crisis ended in June 2009.[4] The second half of 2009 and all of 2010, 2011, 2012, and 2013 were growth years.[5] All official sources forecast continued growth in the US economy for 2014 and 2015. In 2013, the US economy produced 6% more goods and services in real dollar terms than it had in 2007, the last pre-recession year of solid economic growth.[6] Private industry is more productive and more profitable than ever. The stock market Dow Jones Industrial Average "reached yet another record high" on September 19, 2014.[7] For the US economy, things have never been so good. So what's the problem? If the economy is growing, why aren't companies hiring? Why is it so hard for people to find decent jobs?

The simple answer is that the economy has changed, and the private sector simply doesn't need another 9 or 10 million workers to get things done. If it did, it would hire them. It's ridiculous to blame job seekers for not looking hard enough. The jobs just aren't there, and it's increasingly looking like they're not going to be there. That gives us three basic options to choose from in deciding how to run our economy:

A. We can let people stay home and starve—if they have a home. Those who have homes and a partner to support them won't starve, but they will suffer from depression, anxiety, and increased risk of suicide.[8] They are likely to die younger than they otherwise would.[9] Their children will experience more child abuse.[10] Leaving the problem of unemployment to fester is the easiest choice for government and for those of us who still have good jobs, but it is wantonly destructive for society as a whole.

B. We can pay people not to work—in other words, give them welfare. This is better than leaving them to fend for themselves, since it reduces some of the extreme stress placed on people who can't provide for themselves and their families. Programs like in-school free breakfast and lunch, food stamps, housing assistance, and mortgage relief also help. But welfare can lead to many of the same damaging stresses as not helping people at all, and welfare doesn't do anything to prevent the deterioration of people's knowledge and skills.

C. We can put people back to work—by creating jobs. There is no shortage of work to be done that the private sector won't do on its own. The public sector can fix up government buildings, repair our collapsing bridges, lay new water pipes, improve airports, install sidewalks, upgrade roads for safer driving, expand mass transit, build a national broadband network. We can restore wetlands and wildernesses to improve the environment and reduce the risk of catastrophic flooding. Public improvements may not generate immediate profits for the private sector, but they sure do improve things for the public—and lay the foundations for future economic growth.

Put that way, option C seems by far the most sensible option. But that's not some kind of rhetorical sleight of hand. That's just the way it is. The year 2014 is five years into the recovery from the 2008 recession. The average recovery period in the modern era has lasted 58.4 months, or just under 5 years.[11] If we're not at the top of the cycle already, we're almost certainly close to it. A rational policymaker would not wait for the recovery to create another 10 million jobs. A rational policymaker would be planning now for the next recession. The chances are it will come very soon, and almost certainly before 2018. The longest expansion period ever recorded in all of American history—from 1991 to 2001—lasted just 10 years. And the current recovery feels nothing like the 1990s. Five years into the 1990s expansion, the economy was already employing 9.5 million more people than at the pre-recession peak in March 1990, on its way to adding a total of more than 20 million new jobs.[12] If we wait for the economy to create another 20 million jobs on its own, we might be waiting a long time.

Forget about private sector job creation through tax rebates, investment incentives, and all the other freebies that CEOs and industry lobbyists tell us they want. Of course they want them: Who wouldn't want rebates and incentives? But they don't create jobs. They create profits, which is why companies want them. Corporate profits are now higher, both absolutely and as a proportion of national income, than at any other time in US history.[13] Federal Reserve Bank economists estimate that it takes around $125,000 in government stimulus spending to create one job.[14] It is widely accepted, outside rich people circles, that tax cuts are even less effective at creating jobs, if they create any jobs at all.[15] All in all, handouts to the private sector and to individuals may be popular, but they are not very effective at creating jobs. Direct government hiring would be much more efficient—and it would ensure that the workers hired got decent, full-time jobs with good benefits.

According to a January 2012 Congressional Budget Office report, the average federal worker with a high school diploma and some additional education costs the government $45.70 an hour in total compensation (including benefits), or around $90,000 a year.[16] Of this amount, more than $10,000 will come right back to the federal government in taxes, yielding a net cost of at most $80,000 per worker. State governments generally pay lower salaries and thus could expand employment even more efficiently. At $80,000 per worker, it would cost $800 billion per year to create 10 million new federal jobs. That would require a 20% increase in the federal budget. That might sound like a lot, but it's been done before: During World War II and the Korean War, but also in 2008-09.[17] That's right: Instead of bailing out the banks to prevent an economic depression, we could have directly financed the creation of 10 million jobs to prevent an economic depression. It's far from obvious that we made the right choice.

But it wouldn't really take $800 billion in direct government hiring costs to create 10 million new jobs. When new public sector spending is injected into the economy, it generates additional jobs through a multiplier effect: When newly employed people buy groceries, they generate jobs in grocery stores. Those new employees in grocery stores pay taxes, further reducing the overall cost of creating jobs. And of course the more people have jobs, the fewer people collect welfare benefits or (even more costly) end up in jail. The bond rating firm Moody's estimates that the multiplier effect of federal government spending falls in the range of 1.36 to 1.75, meaning that an extra dollar of federal spending increases total national income by $1.36 to $1.75.[18] Back of the envelope calculations suggest that $500 billion in new federal government payrolls would be enough to generate the 10 million new jobs the economy needs. This figure is roughly in line with the estimates derived by University of Massachusetts economists.[19] It is much less than the actual amount spent on the 2008-10 fiscal stimulus that was passed to fight the recession.

Unless the government is going to run deficits forever, expanding payrolls means raising taxes, but taxes for a good cause. At a time when the richest 1% of Americans are taking home record incomes, and the largest corporations are earning record profits, we can realistically expect them to pay additional taxes to make sure that everyone who needs a job has access to a good one. The argument that tax increases kill jobs just won't wash. Even if it were true, it wouldn't justify leaving millions of people unemployed. Poor people need jobs more than rich people need yachts, and the yacht-building industry just isn't big enough to provide the number of jobs we need.

Can we really put millions of people to work on needed public improvements without wasting billions of dollars? First, money spent putting someone in a job instead of on welfare (or in jail) is never wasted money. Second, it's been done before. There's a good chance your local courthouse, library, and post office were built by the Public Works Administration (PWA), your local through roads, water mains, and sewer lines were laid down by the Works Progress Administration (WPA), and your favorite park trails were cut and marked by the Civilian Conservation Corps (CCC)—all New Deal job creation programs. At their height Franklin Roosevelt's New Deal programs gave jobs to more than 3.6 million people out of an adult labor force of just 53 million, or about 6.8% of the labor force. [20] Creating 10 million government jobs for today's adult labor force of 156 million would require a comparable national effort. Creating six million government jobs and letting the spending multiplier do the rest would be easy by comparison.

Whether or not the New Deal ended the Great Depression, it certainly put people back to work. Seven years into the Great Recession, people still need work. Government action on jobs is long overdue. At the current rate of job creation, the number of available jobs will literally never catch up with the growing number of people who need employment, since the population is expanding faster than the number of jobs. And don't forget: Right now, the economy is actually growing. These are the good times. They won't last forever. There is a good chance that by 2016 the United States will experience another recession and a near certainty that the next recession will hit by 2018. If the next President of the United States does not immediately prioritize job creation, that next recession will wreak havoc on an already weak job market. Yes, things can (and will) get even worse.

The private sector has had six years to show it can create jobs. It has shown, very clearly, that it doesn't want or need to. The private sector can and will grow without them. The public sector, by contrast, can and should put people back to work. Job creation should be at the top of every candidate's agenda for 2016. There will never be a consensus on far-reaching progressive goals like saving the environment when more than 10 million Americans need jobs. There are many other important goals for progressives to take on, but first and foremost is unabashed no-holds-barred US government job creation. Any politician who doesn't understand that the ongoing jobs crisis requires direct government intervention should not be taken seriously as a candidate for President of the United States in 2016. The US economy has experienced 11 recessions since 1945. It will eventually experience a twelfth. If the jobs crisis hasn't been solved before it hits, God help us. It will be too late to help ourselves.

2
BUILD AMERICA'S HUMAN INFRASTRUCTURE

The 2000s were the worst decade for job creation ever recorded in US history.
Between 2000 and 2010 the U.S .economy added a grand total of
just two million jobs. That compares with more than 20 million new
jobs created during the infamous 1970s.[1] The American economy had
problems in the 1970s but nothing like the problems of the 2000s.
Ten times as many jobs were created in the 1970s as in the 2000s.
Real median wages for Americans of all ages were higher in the 1970s
than at any time since.[2] In the 1970s the official poverty rate averaged
11.9%. In the years since 1980 the average has been 13.6%. In 2012
it reached 15.0%.[3] Seen from the perspective of someone coming out
of the glorious boom years of the 1950s and 1960s, the 1970s might
have seemed pretty awful. Dispassionately evaluated in retrospect they
seem pretty good, at least economically. Some people even like the
clothes—maybe not the hairstyles, but then you can't have everything.

The big economic problem of the 1970s was inflation. Annual
consumer price inflation hit 12.4% in 1974 and 13.3% in 1979.[4]
Everyone who lived through those days remembers the long lines
at service stations and skyrocketing prices for gasoline. We may not
remember that in 1973-74 the Arab countries withdrew oil from
the world market in protest against US support for Israel in the 1973
Yom Kippur War. In 1978-80 Iranian oil exports were disrupted by
the Iranian revolution and Saddam Hussein's invasion of Iran. In other
words, the biggest economic problem of the 1970s—inflation—was
mainly the result of our foreign policy debacles in the Middle East.
It's no wonder that every President since has focused so much foreign
policy (and military) firepower on the region. The Middle East
killed the presidency of Jimmy Carter just as surely as it killed the
government's commitment to maintaining full employment.

Where did we go wrong? The economics profession doesn't seem to have the answers. It is hard to take conservative economists very seriously when they tell us that the problem today is too much regulation, or too much taxation, and too much government spending. We've done nothing but cut, cut, cut for 40 years with very little to show for it. If government regulation, waste, and inefficiency are destroying the economy now, why were there so many more jobs back in the 1970s when regulations were so much stronger, taxes were so much higher, and the government was so much bigger?

The answer may not be better economics but better sociology. The economics profession is very good at understanding how economies change from year to year but not very good at understanding how societies change from century to century. In the 20th century, the US needed more food, fuel, housing, appliances, machinery, and gadgets of all kinds. People wanted cars and industry wanted trucks. The private sector built them, and market economics made sense. In the 21st century, America doesn't really need more things. Most of us—all except the homeless and the very poor—have too many things. You might need a new car, but you don't need a third, fourth, or fifth car. We have lots of problems with the distributions of things, but we don't need more things. When we do need things, they're usually made overseas. Fewer than 14% of American workers are employed in goods-producing industries.[5]

Sociology tells us that the economy of things is behind us. Ahead is the economy of services and experiences. Some of these services and experiences can be delivered by the private sector. The private sector does a great job when it comes to entertainment, sports, restaurant meals, and shopping malls. Whenever a service provides instant gratification, the private sector is ready to serve us. No one does instant gratification better than corporate America. When services don't involve instant gratification, the private sector does less well. For-profit universities encourage poor families to take on thousands of dollars in debt to buy their children useless online degrees—when they graduate at all.[6] Unregulated health providers sell bogus medical tests that have no basis in science.[7] Corporate prisons with no interest in rehabilitation turn punishment into profit.[8]

It is an axiom of private sector management that what gets measured gets done. And what gets measured is profit. That works fine for cars: A company that makes good cars will make a good profit. It works for restaurants and shopping malls too. But profitability is not a very good guide to school quality. The children of America's elite do not attend for-profit schools.

The reason why profitability is a good guide for cars and restaurants is that the profit motive and instant gratification work very well together. As consumers we are very good at selecting the products and services that give us instant gratification. Companies that are good at providing those products and services prosper. Those that do not fade away. As consumers we are very good at instant gratification but not very good at planning for the long-term future. That should be obvious from our waistlines: Most of us eat for today and regret it tomorrow. At every opportunity we trash our bodies and numb our minds, and it's not much fun to save for a rainy day.

Just as we do not invest enough in our retirement accounts, we do not invest enough in ourselves. Left to make our own decisions, we overspend and underinvest. That's why we have to allow governments to make some kinds of decisions for us. Deep down, we know we need the nanny state. For example, every parent knows that a child is the most precious thing in the world. Parents will give their lives to save their children. Teachers at Sandy Hook even gave their lives to save other people's children. But when it comes to planning statistically for the future success of a child 10 or 20 years down the road, parents tend to underinvest, even though the investment is in their own children: Everyone knows that young children benefit immensely from pre-K education, yet only 52.5% of American children are enrolled in pre-K programs.[9]

Our propensity to underinvest in our children is the reason we developed compulsory free public education more than a hundred years ago. It's also why we should extend free public education for everyone's children from age five down to age three (or earlier) and up through junior college, college, and postgraduate study. Fifty years ago we were moving in both of those directions. The federal Head Start program for three- and four-year-olds was funded in 1965 with initial enrollments of well over half a million children.[10] Federal Pell Grants for higher education were also authorized in 1965 and at the time paid most of the costs of attendance at state universities. Local community colleges were so well funded that most charged only nominal tuition fees.

The country was also moving toward more or less universal health insurance. President Richard Nixon—yes, he of Vietnam and Watergate—proposed a standardized national health insurance plan to Congress in 1971 and again in 1974. Nixon's plan did not include the "individual mandate" of the 2010 Affordable Care Act, but it did propose to make health insurance essentially free for poor and unemployed Americans. Then the 1970s inflation crisis hit, we took a wrong turn, jumped the tracks, and fell off the wagon.

As federal government programs expanded throughout the 1970s, the US faced the perennial choice: consume now or invest for the future. Obviously, we chose to consume. In the mid-1970s we were actively in the process of creating the world's first postindustrial economy based on education, healthcare, and self-improvement, but by the 1980s we had chosen instead to create the world's first postindustrial economy based on entertainment, retail, and food. Imagine if instead we had chosen to continue investing. Between 1964 and 1974 state and local governments created more than 2.4 million new jobs in education.[11] If state and local education jobs had continued to expand at that rate over the next four decades, there would now be 9.6 million more jobs in public education. Employment crisis solved.

Is that a realistic number? Just over 10 million educators are currently employed by state and local governments.[12] Could schools really employ another 9.6 million people? National Center for Education Statistics figures show that the nationwide student–teacher ratio for all schools is 15.9 students per teacher, while the average student–teacher ratio in Manhattan private schools is 7.8 students per teacher.[13] If we wanted every child in America to enjoy the kinds of class sizes that the Manhattan elite buy for their own children, we would have to hire just over 10 million new educators. In other words, if we had continued down the educational path we set for ourselves 50 years ago, we'd be there by now. The 10 million missing educators in the national education statistics are the 10 million educators we didn't hire when we changed course after 1975, and the 10 million missing jobs in today's jobs equation.

It's the same story with health. American medical schools are turning out roughly the same number of doctors now as they were in 1980.[14] But the US population is 37% larger than it was in 1980, and the elderly population is 61% larger.[15] There just aren't enough doctors to go around. It would likely require a 50% increase in the number of practicing doctors to restore the patient access to medical advice that was available in the 1970s. A healthier society with more personalized healthcare would employ even more doctors per person than the US did 40 years ago. A rough estimate is that we should have about twice as many doctors as we actually have practicing in the US today. Similarly with dentists. Amazingly, dental school enrollments are lower today than they were 30 years ago.[16] As a result, high-quality dental care has come to be seen as a luxury for the middle class instead of a basic human right for all. In the 21st century there is no reason for anyone to lose a tooth due to lack of care, but one third of all American adults do not go to the dentist; nearly one quarter are living with untreated cavities.[17]

When late 20th-century U.S.A choose not to invest in education, healthcare, and self-improvement, it doomed early 21st-century

Americans to decades of unemployment, underemployment, and unfulfilled potential. This should come as no surprise. Just like physical infrastructure, human infrastructure moves in long-term historical arcs. Think about the age of the infrastructure we use every day. For example, all of Manhattan's major bridges were built between 1883 and 1936. Most of America's municipal water and sewer systems are 50-100 years old. Our railroads were almost all built before 1950 and the interstate highway network dates to the 1960s. Even America's major airports are now decades old: At least 20 airports or airport buildings are listed on the National Register of Historic Places.[18] We are living off the investments of an earlier era.

When industrial society changed to postindustrial society and it came time to invest more in human infrastructure, we balked. First progress toward the Great Society of President Lyndon Johnson stalled under the Richard Nixon administration in the 1970s. Then in 1981 Ronald Reagan rode in on his high horse and declared on his first day in office that "government is not the solution to our problem; government is the problem." As a result we're now 40 years behind in building the human infrastructure of a 21st-century society. The good news is that we can catch up rapidly if we try. The even better news is that catching up would itself put a lot of people to work. Individual consumers can't build public education and healthcare systems any more than individual commuters can build roads or subways. We have to accept that government is not the problem. We are the problem. Government is the solution.

3
SUPPORT PUBLIC EDUCATION

Reform (noun): a policy that is designed to undermine the effectiveness of a public institution in a way that generates private gains.

Reform (verb): to make something worse.

When did reform become a dirty word? Thirty years of education reform have brought a barren, test-bound curriculum that stigmatizes students, vilifies teachers, and encourages administrators to commit wholesale fraud in order to hit the testing goals that have been set for them.[1] Strangely, reform has gone from being a progressive cause to being a conservative curse. It used to be that good people pursued reform to make the world a better place, usually by bringing public services under transparent, meritocratic, democratically governed public control. Today, reform more often involves firing people and dismantling public services in the pursuit of private gain. Where did it all go so wrong? Who stole our ever-progressing public sector, and in the process stole one of our most effective words for improving it?

At least so far as education reform is concerned, the answer is clear. The current age of education reform can be traced to the landmark 1983 report *A Nation at Risk*, subtitled "The Imperative for Educational Reform." Future dictionaries may mark this report as the turning point when the definition of reform changed from cause to a curse. In 1981 Ronald Reagan's first Secretary of Education Terrel H. Bell appointed an 18-person commission to look into the state of US schools. He charged the commission with addressing "the widespread public perception that something is seriously remiss in our educational system." The commission included 12 administrators, 1 businessperson,

1 chemist, 1 physicist, 1 politician, 1 conservative activist, and 1 teacher. No students or recent graduates. No everyday parents. No representatives of parents' organizations. No social workers, school psychologists, or guidance counselors. No representatives of teacher's unions (God forbid). Just one practicing teacher and not a single academic expert on education.[2]

It should come as no surprise that a commission dominated by administrators found that the problems of US schools were mainly caused by lazy students and unaccountable teachers. Administrative incompetence was not on the agenda. Nor were poverty, inequality, and racial discrimination. *A Nation at Risk* began from the assumption that our public schools were failing. Of course our public schools were failing. Our public schools are always failing. No investigative panel has ever found that our public schools are succeeding. But if public schools have been failing for so long—if they were already failing in 1983 and have been failing ever since—then very few of us alive today could possibly have had a decent education. So who are we to offer solutions for fixing these failing schools? We are ourselves the products of the very failing schools we propose to fix.

Which gets to the point of the matter: For most of the 150-year-history of public education in the US, public schools have done a pretty good job. There is no crisis in public education. There never has been—or at least not until now. This time really is different. This time the issue is not the quality of our public schools. This time the issue is the survival of our public schools *as* public schools. Public schools today face relentless attacks from pro-business conservatives who see US public education budgets as pots of gold to be mined for private gain. In the 2011–12 school year no fewer than 35 states supported for-profit "education management organizations" (EMOs) with taxpayer money; these for-profit EMOs collectively "managed" the education of 462,926 students.[3] These figures from the National Education Policy Center include only for-profit "public" schools and do not include students educated at private schools at public expense through school voucher programs. They are also minimum figures; they include only the schools that the authors of the study could find and identify as being run for-profit providers. There is no centralized database for tracking the privatization of our public schools.

There is also a not-for-profit EMO sector that is roughly equal in size to the for-profit EMO sector. The dirty open secret of not-for-profit EMOs is that most (though not all) of them are essentially just pass-through front operations for profit-making companies. The fine line between not-for-profit and for-profit EMOs is finely delineated in Stephanie Strom's in-depth 2010 report for the *New York Times*.[4] For all practical policy purposes, the for-profit and not-for-profit EMO sectors can be considered one and the same. Putting both together, and assuming that 10% of the sector is not captured in the National Education Policy Center's annual survey, puts the likely number of public school students sitting in for-profit classrooms at over one million. This is still a small proportion of all public school students, but it is growing rapidly. Taken to its rational conclusion, the conservative agenda calls for nothing less than the complete privatization of all public education in America.[5]

The privatization agenda can be very seductive. Students aren't studying? Threaten to fail them and hire private testing companies to keep them in line. Teachers aren't teaching? Threaten to fire them and create private charter schools to replace them. Parents are voters and by definition always right, so empower parents as consumers to buy the education they want for their children. We choose and buy our children's food, clothing, and toys. Why not choose and buy our children's education? Why should government bureaucrats decide what's best for our kids? The conservative agenda will put us in charge of our children's education. What could be wrong with that?

First, our children's education should be in the hands of professionals whose first and only priority is education. Do we really want our children's futures to be in the hands of for-profit corporations? For that matter, do we really want our children's futures to be completely in the hands of their parents? It is a sacrilege in politics to say anything bad about parents, but let's face facts. Collectively, we give our children too much food and too little exercise. We use televisions and computers (sorry, educational videos and learning software) as baby-sitters. Our basements, closets, and garages are filled with piles of junk that pass for toys. Parents are great at love and security but maybe not so great at education. In contrast, public school teachers are full-time professionals who are trained in child development and paid to focus on our children all day (and often unpaid into the night). Sometimes it's best to rely on professionals for things that really matter.

An important principle of professionalism is that professionals should not stand to gain or lose from the decisions they make in carrying out their professional duties. A serious problem in the medical profession is that doctors can make much more money working for the drug companies than working for their patients. A better model is to insulate professionals from financial considerations. Clearly, for-profit schools are dangerous because as for-profit companies they are obliged to care more about their profits than about our children. Ditto companies that provide pre-packaged educational products like standardized tests, test preparation software, pre-packaged lesson plans, and even school lunches. Buyer beware.

Truly public schools insulate educational decision makers from profit motives of all kinds. Unionized schools ensure even higher levels of professionalism by insulating educators themselves from the day-to-day pressures of financial performance. That's not a bad thing. That's a fantastic thing. Union protections reduce the incentives teachers face to give high grades just to keep everyone happy, to push "difficult" children out of their classes, and to teach to the test. Unions ensure that school districts provide appropriate professional training opportunities for teachers and administrators. And unions prevent favoritism in the awarding of raises and promotions, substituting instead the principle of seniority based on experience. In short, a unionized school may not be a perfect school, but it is a professional school.

The second reason that strong public schools are in the national interest is that the most important purpose of public education is not to educate students. It is to build the American nation. Think about it. Why is the government even involved in education? Why not leave parents to pay for their own children's education? We don't feed, bathe, house, and clothe each other's children. Why do we pay others to educate them? The answer is not charity. We have programs to help feed, house, and provide medical care for the children of the poor. But we don't provide these benefits to the children of the rich. We don't even provide free medical care to the children of the rich. But we provide free public education to everyone.

We provide free public education to everyone because education is primarily about good citizenship, not academic learning. All those hours spent in classrooms should be used to help our children grow into happy, productive, moral, responsible, reasonably well-behaved adult citizens who care deeply about our communities, our country, and our world. Subjects like art, music, and theater are just as important for citizenship as are subjects like English, science, and math. Reading, writing, and arithmetic may be necessary skills for life in modern society, but when was the last time you had to diagram a sentence or factor an equation? And if you had to, could you? Even if private companies or charter schools could raise student test scores (and there is no evidence that they do), they cannot shape citizens.[6] Citizens can only be created by committee. And the bigger that committee—the broader our children's education—the better.

Education for citizenship requires the involvement of parents and teachers but also school administrators, elected school boards, parents' groups, teachers' unions, parent-teacher associations, religious congregations, local businesses, sports clubs, community orchestras and playhouses, and all the other stakeholders in society. Children need multiple bases of support in learning how to grow into adulthood. This is where the 1983 report *A Nation at Risk* went tragically wrong. It excoriated the transformation of schools into community centers and sought to reverse the trend. Ever since then, education reform has focused on turning schools into knowledge factories. Teach more, study more, test more. Everything else—less.

The data show that the knowledge factory model of education has done nothing to improve test scores, which have been essentially unchanged since 1971.[7] Countries like Finland that embed schools in the community do much better on standardized tests than we do, and states like Massachusetts that embed schools in the community do much better on standardized tests than do states that focus more on knowledge transfer.[8] Not that success on standardized tests should be the goal of public education. It shouldn't. But if the knowledge factory model doesn't even improve standardized test scores, what is it good for? The obvious answer is: nothing. Worse, the knowledge factory model is absolutely catastrophic for meeting the true goals of education. It destroys them. We don't need schools to disseminate knowledge. We have the internet for that, and before the internet we had books. Most of us learned very little in school.

What we need schools for—strong public schools—is to reproduce America in the next generation. America isn't a place; it's a people. All Americans have a stake in shaping what the its next generation will be like, even people who don't have children. That's why even people who don't have children pay taxes to support public education. Our next President should put the public back into public education. We don't need gimmicky national standards programs. We need national financial support for local public schools, staffed by professionals who know their students and care about their communities.

Enough with false reform. The federal government should entrust states and communities to bring up good citizens, and give them the resources to do so. States should trust their counties, and counties their towns. It may go against political nature to provide funding without demanding measurable outcomes, but good citizenship is not measurable. A progressive President who is not beholden to the for-profit education industry can pull many levers that will return America's public schools to public management in the public service. The for-profit education industry may still be small enough to be beaten in 2016. By 2020 it will almost certainly be too late.

4
EXTEND MEDICARE TO EVERYONE

Medicare for all—that about covers it. A civilized country needs universal healthcare, and the only effective way to provide it is through a government-managed program. The United States already has several government-managed programs, but by far the most effective and most efficient is Medicare. Medicare may not be perfect, but it works, and it works at relatively low cost.[1] Almost every American aged 65 and over is covered by Medicare. If Medicare can deliver basically sound healthcare for the this group—the highest-risk part of the population—it should be able to deliver basically sound healthcare for the rest of us. The idea that government-paid healthcare for people over 65 is normal and ordinary, but government-paid healthcare for people under age 65 is some kind of un-American, communist conspiracy is flat-out ridiculous. Medicare already pays more than 20% of all personal healthcare expenses in the country.[2] It is well on its way to being a universal program. It should be made a universal program.

Medicare is an insurance program in four parts. Part A covers hospital bills, Part B covers doctors' bills. Part C, also known as Medicare Advantage, is an optional private insurance plan that Medicare recipients can choose to receive instead of Parts A and B. Part D, the newest part, is a private insurance plan for prescription drugs.[3]

Medicare needs a lot of work. Private Medicare Advantage plans should be made simpler and more comprehensive. The federal government should take back the right to negotiate Part D drug prices that Congress gave up in 2003.[4] This change alone would save taxpayers tens of billions of dollars per year.[5] Many other tweaks, refinements, and improvements should be made. But the bedrock principle that every American should have inexpensive access to all necessary healthcare should not be a matter for debate. Other civilized countries recognized that healthcare is a basic human right decades ago. Presidents Truman, Nixon, and Clinton all believed in the necessity of universal healthcare and tried to pass legislation to make it a reality. President Obama used his first-term mandate to push the Affordable Care Act (ACA), popularly known as Obamacare, through Congress in 2010. The ACA is better than nothing at all, but it is a Band-Aid for a sucking chest wound. It is too complicated, too expensive, riddled with perverse incentives for insurance companies, and not truly universal in coverage.[6] Worse, many states are simply not cooperating in its implementation.[7]

By contrast, Medicare is straightforward and universal. Everyone is covered, and everyone gets the same minimum coverage. Add-ons are optional. Medicare doesn't cover everything, but it is good enough for most people, most of the time. It is tried and tested, it is cost-effective, and it works.

Medicare was created in 1965 to deal with a simple fact of life: The fact that we're all going to die. Death can be very expensive, and someone has to pay for it. Fortunately or unfortunately (depending on your perspective), it can be difficult to collect from the dead. Thus Medicare. By design, Medicare is an insurance program both for individuals and for hospitals. Individuals are insured against illness. Hospitals are insured against uncollectible bills. This insurance for hospitals is at least as important as insurance for individuals because it reduces the incentive for hospitals to turn people away based on their ability to pay. Hospitals can't legally or ethically refuse to treat dying patients, but they can use many tricks to encourage the riskiest patients go elsewhere. Medicare reduces the risks hospitals face in treating the elderly and thus makes it possible for elderly Americans to get appropriate care.

The need to save hospitals from bankruptcy is the reason Medicare was created to cover the healthcare needs of those most at risk of death.[8] As a result, Medicare covers not only people over age 65 but also people who need regular dialysis to ward off terminal kidney failure, people with ALS (Lou Gehrig's disease), and some other categories of disabled people. In total 53.5 million Americans are covered by Medicare, 44.6 million of them in the program for people aged 65 and over and 9 million due to disability (with some people eligible for both programs).[9] Medicare is not the only government health program, but it is the most universal government health program: Nearly everyone who lives to age 65 will be covered.

Other government-sponsored healthcare programs are less effective at ensuring appropriate care, in part because they are not universal. They also tend to provide less generous benefits than Medicare. The result is that hospitals and physicians can be reluctant to treat people under age 65 without proof of their ability to pay, even in emergency situations. Strategies include aggressive pre-admittance screening procedures, intentionally sloppy diagnoses that fail to detect life-threatening conditions, admitting emergency patients as ordinary patients instead so that they can more easily be discharged, or simply not having staff available who have the expertise to know that a potential patient needs care.[10] Some for-profit hospitals are outright in demanding up-front payment of some fees before they will treat people.[11] While most people with good insurance will never experience such tactics, for poor and poorly insured Americans these kinds of experiences are routine.

The biggest government healthcare program isn't Medicare. It is the joint federal-state program Medicaid, which covers 59.4 million Americans.[12] Medicaid is a means-tested healthcare program for low-income families and individuals. Enrollment is not automatic and many states severely restrict eligibility. Medicaid is not really one national program but a panoply of distinct state programs of differing quality. Coverage is a kind of poverty lottery: In general it is much better to be poor in progressive-leaning states than in conservative-leaning states. The federal government pays the majority of the costs of Medicaid, but states are not required to take the money. As a result, most conservative-controlled states are refusing to fully implement the

Medicaid expansion funded by the ACA.[13] By operating through the Medicaid program, the ACA effectively put control over expanding government health insurance coverage for poor Americans in the hands of the states. The ACA also allows states to set up their own insurance exchanges for the nonpoor. This has further reinforced the fragmentation of the US healthcare system into multiple state systems.

Worse, states tend to pay physicians much less to care for Medicaid patients than the federal government pays them for Medicare patients, making it difficult for Medicaid patients to find doctors. The Kaiser Family Foundation reports that the national average Medicaid physician payment is just two-thirds the level of Medicare physician payments.[14] The result is that many physicians simply decline to accept Medicaid patients.[15] This point was underscored by a much-reported study that showed dramatically increased emergency room usage among people who receive Medicaid.[16] Medicaid is not a vehicle for reducing healthcare costs because Medicaid is so poorly designed that in many cases covering people with Medicaid actually increases healthcare costs. Medicaid is better than nothing as an anti-poverty program, but it is not a good healthcare program. It is no substitute for a true national program like Medicare.

In addition to Medicare and Medicaid, another 19 million Americans are covered by other government health insurance programs.[17] Accounting for people who hold multiple government insurance policies at the same time, just over 100 million Americans are covered by some form of government health insurance.[18] That's nearly one third of the US population and rising. Due to the expansion of Medicaid under the ACA, the increasing number of disabled people, and the aging of the population in general, it is almost certain that by 2016 more than one third of all Americans will be insured directly or indirectly by the United States government. In light of this, two conclusions are obvious. First, the more than 100 million people covered by government health insurance should be consolidated into a single program. Second, the other 200 million Americans should be offered access to that program as well. And the obvious program to offer them is Medicare.

The strength of Medicare is that it combines national funding and program administration with local service and provision of care. Doctors and hospitals accept patients, secure in the knowledge that they will be paid a reasonable fee for their services. Patients can choose their own doctors and hospitals, so they can develop relationships with people they trust from their own communities. Patients also have the ability to trade away their right to choose in exchange for expanded services under Medicare Part C (Medicare Advantage). Medicare Advantage now enrolls 28% of Medicare patients, up from less than 7% a decade ago.[19] Nonetheless, despite financial incentives to switch to Part C, most Medicare enrollees decide to keep traditional Medicare coverage—and with it control over their own healthcare.

Medicare Advantage plans cost more than traditional Medicare coverage because the private insurers who run them have to cover the costs of marketing, shareholder returns, and exorbitant executive salaries.[20] Once these extra costs are factored in, Medicare Advantage providers are unable to compete with traditional Medicare. Medicare Advantage enrollment only rose above 7% after the federal government started to subsidize these plans in 2003. In effect, Medicare enrollees had to be bribed to move over to Medicare Advantage. Without the sweeteners, nearly everyone preferred traditional Medicare. The private sector simply could not generate enough efficiencies to overcome its higher costs and enrollees' preference for control over their own healthcare.

That should be a lesson to the rest of us. The ACA uses the threat of a tax penalty (the "individual mandate") to push everyone under age 65 into employer-sponsored health insurance, Medicaid, or the new health insurance exchanges. All of these systems limit patient choice and put either public or corporate bureaucrats in charge of our healthcare. The argument for bureaucratic control over healthcare—or managed care—is that it is supposed to reduce costs. But the experience of Medicare Part C shows that this is not the case. Medicare Part C Medicare Advantage programs cost, on average, 13% more than traditional Medicare.[21] Even with this 13% subsidy, 72% of Medicare patients turn down the managed care option.

Along with the education system, the healthcare system is a key component of the US human infrastructure. As with our education system, our long-standing traditions of local control and community care should remain bedrock principles of our healthcare system. The strength of our communities is ultimately the strength of our country. Managed care is not community care. The choice between managed care and Medicare is more than a choice between an expensive system that generates corporate profits and an efficient system that serves the public interest. It is a choice between bureaucratic decision making and personal empowerment.

Polls show that at least half and almost certainly more than 60% of Americans support the idea of a single-payer, government-administered health insurance system like Medicare being extended to everyone.[22] Most doctors also support the idea.[23] Considering that traditional Medicare coverage is both cheaper and more desirable than the options offered under the ACA, the simple promise of "Medicare for All" should be a top progressive priority for 2016. The US healthcare system may be broken, but Medicare isn't what broke it. Medicare is what holds it together.

Instead of having to wait until they turn 65, Americans should be enrolled in Medicare at birth, just as most babies now have Social Security numbers put right on their birth certificates. Why not include a Medicare card along with a Social Security card as part of life's welcome packet? All progressives accept the principle that everyone needs healthcare. The only question is how to pay for it. The ACA is a first step in the right direction. The next step should be much more ambitious. If everyone needs healthcare, we should make sure they get it in the most effective way possible. Medicare for all is simple, efficient, and affordable. It is a winning policy for 2016.

5
RAISE TAXES ON TOP INCOMES

Back in the good old days, that is to say the mid-1990s, taxpayers with annual incomes over $500,000 paid federal income taxes at an average effective rate of 30.4%.[1] For 2012, the latest year for which data are available, the equivalent figure was 22.0%.[2] The much-ballyhooed January 1, 2013 tax deal that made the Bush-era tax cuts permanent for all except the very well-off will do little to reverse this trend: The deal that passed Congress only restores pre-Bush rates on the last few dollars of earned income, not on the majority of earned income, on corporate dividends, or on most investment gains.[3] Someone has had a very big tax cut in recent years, and the chances are that someone is not you.

In the 1990s taxes on high incomes were already low by historical standards. Today, they are even lower. The super-rich are able lower their taxes even further through a multitude of tax minimization and tax avoidance strategies.[4] The very tax system itself has in many ways been structured to meet the needs of the super-rich, resulting in a wide variety of situations in which people can multiply their fortunes without actually having to pay tax.[5] In general, it is also much easier to hide income when most of your income comes from investments than when your income is reported on regular W-2 statements from your employer direct to the IRS. Whatever our tax statistics say about the tax rates of the super-rich, we can be sure they are lower in reality.

At the same time that their tax rates are going down, the annual incomes of highly paid Americans are going through the roof. In the 1990s the average income of the top 0.1% of American taxpayers was around $3.6 million. In 2012 it was nearly $6.4 million.[6] And yes, these figures have been adjusted for inflation. Thanks to the careful database work of *Capital in the Twenty-First Century* author Thomas Piketty and his colleagues, it is now relatively easy to track and compare the incomes of the top 1%, 0.1%, and 0.01%. The historical comparisons don't make for pretty reading. Forget the merely well-off 1%. In the 21st century the top 0.1% of American households have consistently taken home more than 10% of all the income in the country, up from 3% in the 1970s.[7] And these figures only include realized income: that is to say, income booked and reported to the tax authorities. If you own a company that doubles in value but you don't sell any shares, you don't have any income. Ditto land, buildings, airplanes, yachts, artwork, coins, stamps, etc.

High inequality plus low taxes equals fiscal crisis. The rich are taking more and more money out of the economy, but they are not returning it in the form of taxes. The result is that the US government no longer has the resources it needs to properly govern the country. The country needs universal preschool, universal healthcare, and a massive government-sponsored jobs program. The country needs a complete renewal of its crumbling human and physical infrastructure. The country needs funds for everything from the cleanup of atomic waste in Hanford, Washington to improvements at the National Zoo in Washington, D.C. And the country needs higher taxes on today's higher incomes to pay for it all.

In 2010 the United States government collected a smaller proportion of the nation's total national income in income taxes than at any time since 1950.[8] That figure has since rebounded, but it is still well below the average from 1996-2001. Under current law the federal income tax take is projected to rise from the historic low of 6.1% in 2010 to 8.6% of national income in 2016. This is an improvement over recent years, but it is still far below the average of 9.5% for the years 1998-2001, the last time the federal government actually ran a budget surplus.[9]

The top marginal tax rate on the highest incomes is now 39.6%, as it was in the 1990s. This is still a far cry from the 50% top tax bracket of the 1970s or the 70% top tax bracket of the 1960s, never mind the 91-92% top tax brackets of the 1950s.[10] The return to 1990s levels is a good start, but the next President should push to go much farther back because the tax system has been moving in the wrong direction for a very long time. High incomes are much higher than they ever were and people with high incomes pay much less tax than at almost any time in our modern history. The result, unsurprisingly, has been the enormous concentration of income among a small, powerful elite documented by Piketty in *Capital in the Twenty-First Century* but no less obvious for all to see.

The concentration of income among a powerful elite may be very good for members of that elite, but it is bad for our society, bad for our democracy, and even bad for our economy. Socially, highly concentrated incomes undermine our national institutions and warp our way of life. For example, people who can afford to send their children to exclusive private schools cease to care for the health of public education, or they erect barriers to separate "their" public schools from everyone else's public schools. Similarly, people who can afford the very best private healthcare care little about ensuring high-quality public healthcare. People who fly private jets care little about congestion at public airports. People who drink imported bottled water care little about the poisoning of rivers and underground aquifers. Enormous differences in income inevitably create enormous distances between people. The United States is starting to resemble the fractured societies of Africa and Latin America, where the rich live in gated "communities" with armed guards who enforce the exclusion of the lower classes—except to allow them entry as maids and gardeners.

These nefarious effects of inequality can already be seen in America's sunbelt cities, where there are fine gradations of gated communities: armed guards for the super-rich, unarmed guards for the merely well-off, keypad security for the middle class, and on down the line to the unprotected poor. We should be ashamed, one and all.

Politically, highly concentrated incomes threaten the integrity of American democracy by fostering corruption of all kinds. When the income differences between regulators and the industries they regulate are small, we can count on regulators to look after our interests. But when industry executives make two or three (or ten) times as much as regulators, it is almost impossible to prevent corruption. Even where there is no outright corruption, it is impossible for regulators to retain talented staff. People will take modest income cuts to work in secure public sector employment. They will not take massive income cuts. Those who do are often just doing a few years on the inside so they can better evade regulation when they go back to the private sector. When doing a few years on the inside includes serving in Congress merely as way to get a high-paying job as a lobbyist, we are in serious trouble.

Along with highly concentrated incomes come vote buying and voter suppression. When the stakes are so high, people will play dirty. No one knows how many local boards of one kind or another around the country have been captured by local economic interests, but the number must be very large.

Economically, highly concentrated incomes ensconce economic privilege, suppress intergenerational mobility, and can ultimately lead to the total breakdown of the free market as a system for efficiently driving production and consumption decisions. Privilege is perpetuated by excessive incomes because with enough money the advantages of wealth overpower any amount of talent and effort on the part of those who are born poor. Nineteenth-century English novels were obsessed with inheritance and marriage because in that incredibly unequal society birth trumped everything else. Twenty-first-century America has now reached similar levels of income concentration among a powerful elite. To make this point graphically clear, a family with a billion-dollar fortune that does absolutely no planning to avoid the 40% tax on large estates and no paid work whatsoever can comfortably take out $15 million a year to live on (after taxes, adjusted for inflation) in perpetuity until the end of history—while still growing the estate. That's how mind-bogglingly large a billion-dollar fortune is.[11]

But probably the least recognized impact of high inequality on our economy is that it severely impairs the efficient operation of the free market itself. Market pricing is at its core a mechanism for rationing. The market directs limited resources to the places where they command the highest prices.

The basic idea of rationing by price is that prices encourage people to carefully weigh their purchases against each other—in other words, to economize. In an economy where everyone earns roughly the same income, rationing by price works just fine for most goods. People take care of their necessities first. Then they can choose whether to spend their extra money on eating out, taking vacations, renovating their homes, or saving up to buy something big like a boat. Because all of these goods are priced in the same currency, people can directly compare their values against each other. And if everyone has roughly the same amount of money to spend, market prices represent roughly the same values for different people. If you and I have the same income, a $20 restaurant meal means as much to me as it does to you.

Problems set in when incomes are very unequal. For people with extraordinarily high incomes, prices become meaningless. What does a $20 restaurant meal mean to someone who makes $20 million a year? Nothing. The result is incredible waste as the market economy no longer forces people to economize. When rich people accumulate dozens of cars, maintain yachts they only use once a year, or have servants order fresh-cut flowers every day for houses they rarely visit, they are wasting resources that could be put to much better use by other people. Waste like this invalidates the foundational principle of modern economics: that the market maximizes the total utility of society. That principle only holds if a dollar has the same meaning for you as it does for me. Highly concentrated incomes undermine the whole idea of the market as an economy—that is, as something that economizes.

And that is the strongest argument for much higher taxes on higher incomes. There are many ways to reduce inequality, but the simplest and most efficient way is through taxation. The goal of income taxes should be to tilt the field so that earning an after-tax dollar means just as much to a CEO as to a fast food worker. That's why a 90% marginal tax on incomes over a million dollars is entirely appropriate. For a poor person who pays no income tax, a $20 restaurant meal costs $20. That person must make a real sacrifice to eat out. For a CEO with a 90% marginal tax rate, a $20 restaurant meal costs $200 in before-tax income. That may not be a huge sacrifice for someone who makes several million dollars a year, but it does change the equation. A CEO may not hesitate to eat out, but may hesitate to buy a private jet when flying business class will suffice.

To be sure, we need higher taxes on higher incomes to raise money for government. But we also need higher taxes on higher incomes just to make the economy work properly. That's why the economy worked so much better in the high-tax 1950s and 1960s than it has since. The ultimate goal of income taxes should be to make money as meaningful to a millionaire as it is to you or me. If we can't quite get there in the next few years, we can certainly get closer than we are. One of President Obama's most important accomplishments has been to set us on the path toward economic sanity by raising taxes on the highest incomes. The next President should build on this legacy—and in a big way.

6
REFINANCE SOCIAL SECURITY

Like the crisis in Medicare, the crisis in Social Security is a staple of conservative political punditry. The latest projections are that Medicare will go bankrupt in 2030 and Social Security in 2033.[1] The word "bankrupt" here is a bit of a misnomer. What these dates really represent are the dates on which Medicare and Social Security will start becoming net burdens on the federal budget instead of net contributors to the federal budget (according to the arcane accounting rules by which these programs are governed). The so-called Social Security and Medicare trust funds are little more than accounting devices, as even most conservatives agree.[2] But the Social Security and Medicare programs themselves are core functions of government that together consume over 40% of total government expenditure. Surely they are indispensable parts of whatever it is that a government does, and should be financed as such.

Who pays for the core functions of government? Conservatives are fond of pointing out that most income taxes are paid by the rich, or at least by the well-off. Technically speaking, they are correct. More than half of all personal income tax is paid by households with incomes of over $200,000 a year.[3] Most of the rest is paid by households in the top half of the income distribution. Conservatives are also fond of pointing out that many households pay no personal income tax at all. Again, technically speaking, they are correct. In most years almost half of all households pay no personal income tax, most (but not all) of them relatively poor households.[4] Mitt Romney was essentially correct about the bottom 47% of American household that pay little or no income tax.[5]

Mitt Romney was right, that is, about income tax. If you don't have income, you don't pay income tax. For the 18 million Americans who want jobs but don't have jobs, not paying income tax is the least of their worries.[6] Ditto retired people getting by on Social Security and single parents caring for young children. Then there are the people who work but who earn so little that their tax credits outweigh their tax liabilities. Due to the Earned Income Tax Credit (EITC), introduced by President Gerald Ford and greatly expanded under President Ronald Reagan, many Americans actually get money when they file their taxes.[7] Working at or just above the federal minimum wage of $7.25 an hour it can be hard to make enough money to have any personal income tax liability. The EITC is in effect a federal program that subsidizes low-wage employment through the tax system.

But nearly everyone who works for a living pays taxes. They're just not called income taxes. They're called payroll taxes, or FICA (Federal Insurance Contributions Act) taxes. There are two FICA taxes. The main FICA tax is a 12.4% tax on wage income up to $117,000 a year. This is known as the Old Age, Survivors, and Disability Insurance (OASDI) tax or Social Security tax. Half of the Social Security tax is paid directly by the employee and the other half is paid by the employer on the employee's behalf. The maximum amount of wages that are subject to taxes—$117,000 in 2014—is known as the Social Security wage base or taxable maximum. Wages over the taxable maximum are not subject to Social Security tax. The taxable maximum rises slowly over time according to a formula based on average wages. The second FICA tax is a 2.9% tax on all wage income. This is known as the Hospital Insurance (HI) or Medicare tax. Like the Social Security tax, the Medicare tax is split 50-50 between employees and employers. Unlike the Social Security tax, the Medicare tax is paid on all wages.[8]

Taking both Social Security and Medicare taxes into account, the total combined FICA payroll tax load is 15.3%of wage income on all wages up to $117,000, dropping to 2.9% of all wage income over $117,000. There are no deductions and no exemptions. Everyone who works, pays. [9]

Unlike personal income taxes, with FICA taxes the more you make the less you pay. A person who makes $117,000 pays $17,901 in FICA taxes. A person who earns twice as much—$234,000—pays $21,294. That lucky high-wage person has twice the income but pays just 19% more in taxes. If that seems unfair, spare a tear for the two-earner family. A married couple in which each partner earns $117,000 pays a total of $35,802 in FICA taxes ($17,901 each), while a single person who earns $234,000 all alone pays $21,294 in FICA taxes. The married couple pays 68% more than the single person. That's right: The FICA tax system has a built-in marriage penalty. Though reducing the marriage penalty in income taxes was a major rhetorical focus of the 2001 and 2003 Bush tax cuts, there has been no talk whatsoever in political circles about reducing or eliminating the marriage penalty in FICA taxes.

The FICA tax system shatters Mitt Romney's suggestion that nearly half of all Americans are spongers and scroungers. All working Americans pay substantial taxes, and when it comes to FICA taxes the poorest pay the most. The only people who don't pay FICA taxes don't pay them for the simple reason that they don't have jobs. And the US FICA payroll tax system is perhaps the most regressive major tax in the entire developed world. The richest 1% of American households pay an average FICA tax rate of just 2.2%.[10] Their average FICA tax is even lower than the 2.9% minimum because much of their income comes from investments, which are not subject to FICA taxes. Mitt Romney's 2011 FICA tax rate was presumably 0%, since he did not report any income from wages, salaries, or tips whatsoever.[11]

How important are FICA taxes? All told, FICA taxes bring in more than $1 trillion a year and account for more than one third of all federal government revenue.[12] That's almost as much as the personal income tax and about three times as much as the corporate income tax. The federal government could not operate without the income it receives from FICA taxes.

Because the two FICA taxes are called the Social Security tax and the Medicare tax, people tend to think of them as funding these two programs. In a sense they do. But the connection between FICA and these programs is grounded in legislative history, not in economic reality. In economic reality, caring for the elderly and disabled is a primary function of government. The United States spends more than $800 billion on Social Security and $500 billion a year on Medicare, much more than on defense ($620 billion) and diplomacy ($50 billion).[13] While it is true that the original FICA Social Security tax was created by the same 1935 legislation that created Social Security, the year 1935 was a long time ago and the process that tied them together was actually a paperwork error. And Medicare didn't even come into existence until 1966.

The fundamental flaw crept in when the Social Security Act of 1935 (of which FICA is part) was making its way through Congress. The Roosevelt administration proposed a system of old-age insurance that would cover all blue-collar manual workers and some white-collar office workers—those who made less than $3,000 a year (equivalent to just over $50,000 today).[14] The system was intended to cover all bone fide working-class workers but to exclude managers and executives, who could be expected to plan for their own retirements. Congress mangled the $3,000 limit contained in the Roosevelt plan. Instead of legislating that only working-class workers would receive Social Security benefits while excluding white-collar employees earning over $3,000 a year, Congress extended Social Security benefits to everyone who earned a paycheck, no matter how large.

The result was that all workers came to be covered by Social Security old-age insurance. The $3,000 eligibility test that Roosevelt had proposed to separate working-class office workers from managers and executives was sidestepped but not forgotten. Instead Congress used $3,000 as a limit on the amount of income that would be subject to Social Security taxes. This limit, which has risen to $117,000 in 2014, is now known as the taxable maximum. As a result, Roosevelt's system for providing old age support to ordinary bona fide workers funded by a flat tax on the wages of ordinary bona fide workers was turned into a Congressional system for providing old age support to all workers, funded by a regressive tax on the wages of all workers.

The regressive nature of Social Security taxes makes them profoundly unfair. Important taxes that support core government services should be based on taxpayers' ability to pay. The personal income tax is highest on high incomes. The corporate income tax focuses on profitable companies, not loss-making companies. The FICA payroll taxes are the only major taxes that systematically decline as ability to pay increases. Until 1994 both FICA taxes were completely regressive, with high-earners paying nothing on their wages over the taxable maximums. Then as part of President Bill Clinton's first-term Deficit Reduction Act the taxable maximum was removed for the smaller FICA tax that is nominally earmarked for Medicare. As a result all wages at all levels are now subject to the 2.9% Medicare tax, while only wages under $117,000 are subject to the larger 12.4% Social Security tax.

It's too bad that Clinton didn't push to remove the taxable maximum from all FICA taxes back in 1994. Estimates are that removing the $117,000 taxable maximum would generate an additional $100 billion a year in federal revenue, all of it from relatively high-income tax-payers.[15] Even more income could be generated if FICA taxes were extended to investment income as well as earned income. If we want to reduce the federal deficit from its recent record levels, surely it would be fairer to do so by extending the same FICA taxes to everyone than by cutting food stamps or laying off federal workers. Better to flatten FICA than to flatten future benefits for people who depend on Social Security. A progressive FICA tax (in which low earners paid lower tax rates) would be even fairer.

The progressive political agenda doesn't always have to be about higher taxes. A flat FICA payroll tax system would not dramatically alter the federal government's budget position. An extra $100 billion would be very welcome, but in a $3.5 trillion budget it would not be decisive. What the progressive agenda always has to be about is fairness. The current regressive FICA system is a poke in the eye of all working Americans who aren't lucky enough to make six-figure incomes. It is a poke in two eyes for dual-earner families. It is a poke in the eye for everyone who works for a living while other people live off their investments.

Congress made a mistake in 1935 when it legislated the original taxable maximum for Social Security. That mistake has stood for 80 years. No one who voted on it is alive today. We should not forever be prisoners to the partisan politics of the past. A flat tax for Social Security would be a fair tax for Social Security, and it would sufficiently refinance the program as to keep it technically solvent according to its internal accounting rules (if that matters) for a long time to come. What Bill Clinton did for the Medicare tax in 1993, the next President can promise to do for the Social Security tax after the 2016 election. Who knows—maybe the next President could go one step further. A progressive payroll tax would be even more ... progressive? Either way, a flat FICA would be a good place to start.

7
TAKE DOWN
WALL STREET

If the global financial crisis has taught us anything about finance, it has taught us not to trust the big Wall Street investment banks. The banks created the crisis, demanded a worldwide government bailout, then rapidly returned to excessive profitability. Six years after the crisis, millions of ordinary Americans are still mired in loss (job loss, house loss, asset loss), but after a brief setback in 2008 the banks quickly recovered. They have been making money hand over fist ever since. While wages have stagnated in the rest of the economy, the average New York banker's bonus rose to $164,530 in 2013. That's on top of an average base salary of around $200,000.[1] Wall Street bankers now make more than five times the average New York City salary, compared with less than two times the average in 1981.[2] It seems Wall Street banking is nice work, if you can find it.

The bankers' ball almost came to an end in September, 2008. Investment banks Merrill Lynch, Lehman Brothers, and American International Group (AIG) all collapsed within a few days of each other. Together these three firms owed massive sums of money to the remaining Wall Street banks. If those interbank debts had gone unpaid, the rest of the Wall Street investment banks would have been dragged under as well. Investment bank Goldman Sachs has long been viewed as having the strongest finances of the big Wall Street banks and among the most careful and sophisticated risk management practices. Yet even Goldman "would have been a goner if the Fed didn't throw it a life preserver by paying off AIG's credit default swaps at 100 cents on the dollar and giving Goldman bank-holding-company status, which allowed it to borrow from the Federal Reserve at near-zero interest rates."[3]

The end result? Goldman Sachs not only survived the 2008 crisis with a $2.3 billion profit for the year, but then went on to make a $13.4 billion profit in 2009. It has been profitable ever since.

In the last days of September, 2008 Wall Street pulled off the most audacious raid on the public purse ever contemplated. Treasury Secretary Hank Paulson threatened Congress with financial armageddon and a second Great Depression if it did not immediately provide $700 billion to bail out the remaining investment banks with "very cheap capital."[4] When Republicans in the House of Representatives balked at the price and the process, House Democrats rode to the rescue. Despite the fact that the bill gave extraordinary funding (and powers) to a Republican Secretary of the Treasury to bail out big Wall Street banks, the Emergency Economic Stabilization Act of 2008 was carried by overwhelming Democratic support. The bank bailout was popular with neither Democratic nor Republican voters. "The financial crisis and government-sponsored bank bailout of late 2008 sent trust in government to new lows across party lines," according to a Pew Research report.[5] It took Congress less than one week to give Paulson the $700 billion he requested—roughly equal to the entire annual budget of the Department of Defense.

With the creation of Paulson's $700 billion Troubled Asset Relief Program (TARP) the investment banks' financial armageddon was averted. From the brink of bankruptcy the biggest of the big Wall Street investment banks have bounced back to record profitability. For the rest of the United States, the second Great Depression was not averted. It is ongoing. Just ask the 16.5 million people who are currently unemployed or completely frozen out of the labor market[6]— or the 7.1 million who want full-time employment but can only find part-time jobs.[7] The banking recession is over and the profits recession is over, but the ordinary people's recession goes on.

Why did the United States government bail out the banks instead of stimulating the economy as a whole? At the time that Hank Paulson was nominated to become Secretary of the Treasury in 2006, he was the CEO of the most powerful investment bank on Wall Street, Goldman Sachs. He spent almost his entire private sector career at the firm, acquiring a fortune of some $600 million in the process. He had to sell his Goldman Sachs stock when he became Treasury Secretary, but he didn't have to sell his Goldman Sachs mindset. Hank Paulson brought with him to government the knowledge, prejudices, and ways of thinking of a powerful Wall Street insider. Once a banker, always a banker.

Or perhaps that should be once a gambler, always a gambler. Hank Paulson didn't come out of the staid world of the community banker, making small loans to local businesses. He came out of the big business of Wall Street investment banking. It has often been said that Wall Street operates on the principle of "heads we win, tails you lose." Of course it's not as simple as that. But it's not very much more complicated.

Once upon a time investment banking meant finding financing for long-term investments in industry and infrastructure that could not be met through ordinary bank loans. Those days are long gone. Today the time horizon of the investment banks is very short. Sometimes it can be mind-bogglingly short. For example, big banks now "co-locate" their trading computers in the same rooms as the computers used by the stock exchanges to execute trades.[8] This allows them see stock prices a few milliseconds before the rest of the world, since even electronic signals take time to get from the stock exchange to your computer. Their co-located electronic trading platforms give investment banks the opportunity to snatch up attractive offers before real investors ever get to see them. The bankers themselves don't even see them. Their pre-programmed computers—installed literally on the same racks as the stock exchange computers—trade against you automatically.

Automated electronic trading is the technological cutting edge of what investment banks do, but most of their activities fit the same pattern. Investment banks make enormous profits by skimming pennies off the top every time financial instruments are issued, traded, or retired. They may make mere fractions of a penny. But all those fractions add up. It's like the plot of *Superman III* but for real. Unlike the Richard Pryor character in the film version, the big banks can double or triple their tiny gains by working with money that they borrow overnight at very low short-term interest rates from the Federal Reserve. They also lend these funds out to companies for a few days or weeks at a time on a variety of financial markets. Again, the pennies add up. Bloomberg estimates that the big banks made $13 billion between 2008 and 2010 by taking advantage of special below-market-rate Federal Reserve loans.[9] With subsidies like this, investment banks are essentially money manufacturing assembly lines. They practically print money. They make profits that are inconceivable in any other line of business. And they make them consistently, year in and year out—until there's a crisis.

That's where the gambling comes in. Under ordinary conditions, the investment banking business model results in a consistent, almost risk-free flow of ill-gotten gains. In a normal year, investment banks can't avoid making money. It takes serious employee fraud or systems failure to bring down an investment bank. But when a crisis hits, short-term interest rates shoot up. Companies that used to roll over their routine obligations start to have trouble finding new financing. Investors who sold options can't deliver the goods. Stock prices start to move unpredictably. And investment banks collapse.

The big Wall Street investment banks make their money by playing an endless casino game in which they reliably win millions of small bets but occasionally lose big—very big. In the 2007-09 financial crisis the losses were so severe that every major investment bank on Wall Street should have collapsed. In reality, every one of them did collapse. They only stayed in business because Treasury Secretary Hank Paulson and Federal Reserve Chairman Ben Bernanke came to their rescue.

In March 2008 investment bank Bear Sterns collapsed. Except it didn't collapse. It was rescued by an emergency loan from the Federal Reserve and then sold to J.P. Morgan Chase. Investors who owned Bear Sterns stock in their retirement funds lost nearly everything. Bear Sterns bondholders and counterparties—that is, the investment banks that had lent money to Bear Sterns—lost pretty much nothing. Then in September 2008 investment bank Merrill Lynch collapsed. Again federal financing was used to underwrite a fire sale, this time to Bank of America. Again, the bondholders and counterparties— the other investment banks—lost pretty much nothing. Also in September 2008 Lehman Brothers collapsed. Unlike Bear Sterns and Merrill Lynch, Lehman brothers actually declared bankruptcy. Within hours the Federal Reserve stepped in to provide $138 billion in emergency financing to make sure that Lehman's obligations to its trading counterparties—the other investment banks—were paid that night. Ordinary investors in Lehman Brothers lost nearly everything.

Also in September 2008 AIG collapsed. This time the Federal Reserve stepped in before the company declared bankruptcy, lending AIG $85 billion in a sweetheart deal. When the Congressional bank bailout money came through, Secretary Paulson gave AIG a further $45 billion subsidy. And the list goes on. The US Treasury gave $45 billion to Citigroup, $45 billion to Bank of America, and smaller amounts to other banks and financial firms. The Federal Reserve lent similar amounts, more quietly and with no legislative strings attached.[10] Without support from the Treasury and the Federal Reserve, every one of the big Wall Street investment banks would have disappeared in 2008, and good riddance.

To be clear, most of the bailout money has been repaid—with interest.[11] Contrary to popular perception, the bank bailouts didn't just give money to the banks. It lent money to the banks, albeit at subsidized interest rates and with extremely favorable tax treatment.[12] Put that way, maybe it doesn't seem that bad.

Except that it is that bad. The modern investment banking business model is based on levying a small but continuous tax on everything else that happens in the economy. It is in effect a financial transactions tax, but instead of the tax being collected by the government it is collected by a cabal of big Wall Street banks. Without government support the investment banks' private financial transactions tax would not be sustainable. When a recession hits and tax revenues decline, governments stay in business by borrowing heavily. Investment banks that levy a financial transactions tax must be able to do the same—or collapse into bankruptcy. That is how recessions turn into financial crises. Recessions occur in the real economy. Financial crises occur among big investment banks. Countries with solid banking regulation, like Canada and Germany, have recessions just like the United States does, but they don't have financial crises. No Wall Street, no crisis.

The 2008 financial crisis came almost a year after the beginning of the recession in 2007. The financial crisis didn't cause the recession. The recession caused the financial crisis. Without government subsidized financing for Wall Street, it would have been the last financial crisis. Game over for the investment banks. We could wait for the next recession to do the banks in, but why? There is an easy way to kill the investment banking business model right now—and prevent the next financial crisis from happening at all. Instead of letting the investment banks collect a private financial transactions tax, we can close the casino by enacting a public financial transactions tax.

A federal financial transactions tax would raise between $83 billion and $132 billion under a range of scenarios examined by the Congressional Research Service.[13] It would also kill the goose that lays Wall Street's golden eggs. Or to be more accurate: It would draft her into the public service. If the next President has the courage to push a financial transactions tax through a reluctant Congress, be prepared to hear some very loud squealing. But it won't be the goose squealing. It will be the bankers.

8
MAKE IT EASY TO JOIN A UNION

On Valentine's Day 2014 Volkswagen offered a sweetheart deal to the United Automobile Workers (UAW) union: Please come represent workers at our assembly plant in Chattanooga, Tennessee. Pressured by its German unions, Volkswagen offered its American workers a German-style works council through which workers could participate in decision-making at the plant. Volkswagen executives reassured their workers that unionization would not affect the future of the plant and quietly but clearly supported a pro-union vote.[1]

The Chattanooga workers voted no by a margin of 712-626.

Clearly, unions are not very popular in Tennessee. Still, the UAW and the American union movement have some reason to be hopeful. Unions polled better in Tennessee in 2014 than President Obama did in 2012. Obama won just 39% in the state's votes in the 2012 election, whereas the UAW managed 47% of Volkswagen workers' votes in 2014. Maybe that's not so bad for a bunch of out-of-towners from Detroit.

The really strange thing about the UAW defeat is not that it lost the union representation vote but that in the union representation campaign it faced many of the same opponents as President Obama faced in the general election. Tennessee Governor Bill Haslam, Tennessee's junior US Senator Bob Corker, and ubiquitous Washington insider Grover Norquist all vociferously opposed the unionization of Volkswagen's Chattanooga plant. After the UAW's defeat, Tennessee's senior US Senator Lamar Alexander weighed in to remind everyone that Tennessee workers "have decided in almost every case that they are better off union-free. The UAW may not like this, but that is the right of employees in a right-to-work state like Tennessee."[3]

Tennessee's political establishment played a full court press against union representation in Chattonooga.

Why are big-time, nationally prominent state politicians like Haslam, Corker, and Alexander getting involved in a local workplace decision about the union representation of a small number of workers at a single automobile plant? Politicians don't usually try to influence other private workplace decisions at private companies. Their involvement is even more (rhetorically) mysterious considering that Tennessee is, as Senator Alexander says, a "right-to-work" state. You would think that the right to work would include a right to be left alone in your workplace to make your own decisions about union representation. Sadly, no. Living in a "right-to-work" state doesn't even give you a right to work. In Tennessee, only 55.6% of the working-age population has a job of any kind, compared to 58.6% for the country as a whole.[4] Work is as hard to find in "right-to-work" states as anywhere else.

No, in the business-friendly parlance of conservative America the "right to work" means the "right not to join a union or pay union dues despite the fact that your co-workers have democratically voted for union representation." Under federal law, once a union has won the right to represent the workers in a workplace, it has a duty of representation to fairly and without prejudice represent all workers in that workplace, whether or not they are union members.[5] In "right-to-work" states, recognized unions must fairly represent even those workers who refuse to join them or even to pay modest representation fees. Given the legal duty of fair representation, the problem with granting workers the dubious "right to work" is obvious: Why pay union dues when you are legally entitled to most of the benefits of union representation for free? This is the classic free rider problem. No union can survive for long in a "right-to-work" environment. Inevitably, workers who are facing financial difficulties, lazy about paying their dues, or just plain jerks decide it would be easier not to pay dues than to pay them.

Contrary to conservative opinion, unions are not secret societies dripping in undisclosed private wealth. They are highly regulated membership organizations that are subjected to exceptional levels of public scrutiny. The right to work in "right-to-work" states is a right to freeload on your coworkers who pay union dues so you don't have to. This is a right generously granted to workers in 24 states, including all 11 states of the Old Confederacy.[6] In 2012 and 2013 labor heartland states Indiana and Michigan joined the "right to work" club, though Indiana's law is the subject of an ongoing legal battle.[7] Federal law explicitly gives states the power to pass "right-to-work" laws if they so choose, and increasingly states are doing so. Conservative organizations place the number of states that meet their criteria for being considered right-to-work states at 24 and growing.[8]

There seems no point in conservative politicians mobilizing national business support to defeat a union representation vote in a "right-to-work" state like Tennessee. Even if the UAW had won the vote, any Volkswagen worker could simply refuse to pay dues to the UAW—with no negative consequences. Come to think of it, there seems no point in anti-union workers voting no. If they were really anti-union they would vote for the union, then not join and consequently not pay any fees, despite enjoying nearly all the benefits of union representation. After all, imagine if people could collect all the benefits of American citizenship without paying taxes. How many would voluntarily join the tax-me club? The likely answer is: not many. Not surprisingly, just 3.4% of Tennessee's private sector workers are union members.[9] Almost certainly most of these 73,000 workers work in industries that are not subject to state "right-to-work" laws: railroads, aviation, and certain business activities related to the federal government, which are beyond the reach of state law.

The story is the same all across the South, and increasingly in the rest of the country as well. A huge industry has grown up around advising companies and governments on how to defeat unions. The aggressively vituperative vilification of unions by conservatives and business groups borders on hate speech. But if conservatives hate unions, shouldn't progressives love them? Conservative politicians and political operatives pulled out all the stops to convince Chattanooga Volkswagen workers to reject UAW representation. Where were the progressive politicians and political operatives?

Notably absent.

And that's how it should be. Union representation votes are no place for party politics. In fact, the UAW initially asked the National Labor Relations Board to set aside the February 14 vote against union representation on the grounds that it was unduly influenced by inappropriate political intimidation, though it later withdrew its appeal.[10] On the other side of the debate, the stridently anti-union National Right to Work Legal Defense Foundation actively supports the politicization of union representation campaigns. It prepared a legal brief on behalf of five anti-union Volkswagen workers in Chattanooga defending political interference in union representation votes. The brief claimed that the UAW "proceeds from the misguided premise that it is objectionable if any entity campaigned or spoke against the union in the election. While this belief may reflect how elections are conducted in Venezuela or North Korea, it does not reflect how elections are conducted in this free nation."[11]

Leaving aside the issue of Venezuela's democracy, the National Right to Work Legal Defense Foundation and others who share its point of view fail to recognize that union representation votes are nothing like national elections. Unions are membership organizations. It is hard to see why nonmembers should be involved at all. It is even difficult to see why companies should be involved at all. Volkswagen aside, the US business community is vehemently anti-union for the obvious reason that unions empower workers vis-à-vis their employers. Few American employers are as hands-off as Volkswagen when it comes to union representation votes. But representation is a matter for the workers to decide, not for their employers. Once workers have professional union representation, employers have a right to professional bargaining representation as well. For employers to hire professional union-busting firms to prevent their workers from joining a union seems patently unfair.[12] It seems even more unfair for elected political leaders to seek to influence union representation votes.

Maybe the National Right to Work Legal Defense Foundation is right. Maybe union representation votes should be more like national elections. National elections are held on a regular basis every two years. The people who want to represent you merely have to fill out some pro forma paperwork to appear on the ballot. It is strictly illegal to seek to intimidate, threaten, or coerce voters. Crucially, in a democracy all citizens must pay the taxes imposed by their elected representatives—even if they voted for a different representative, never voted, or never registered to vote. Even people who are not eligible to vote still have to pay taxes. For unions used to dealing with ruthless and well-funded opponents, a system as simple and transparent as a national election would be a blessing beyond their wildest dreams. Every two years workers at all large companies could simply be asked: "which of these candidates do you want to represent you?" Any person or organization that registered as a candidate could run, perhaps including the employer itself. Workers could decide.

After a workplace election, all workers should be held responsible for abiding by the outcome. If the majority votes for a union that charges dues, all workers should be forced to pay their dues. Minority protections might allow workers to opt out of some union programs on moral grounds, but these should be the exception, not the rule. If a majority of workers vote in a fair workplace election free from company or outside intimidation that they would prefer not to join a union, let the unions take their lumps and come back in two years for a rematch. Regular elections for workplace representation would require a whole new approach to labor law in the United States. Given the enormous influence businesses have over politics, democratic reforms like these are unlikely to pass new legislation in this or any future Congress. But it is hard to argue with the idea that workers should be able to vote in a secure, democratic way about whether or not they want union representation, free of coercion from employers, politicians, or even Grover Norquist.

For a time the labor unions themselves supported a much more limited fix to the union election problem: the Employee Free Choice Act (EFCA).[13] The EFCA would have enshrined the "card check" system whereby unions can be empowered to represent workers when over 50% of the workers at a plant sign a card requesting union representation, though the national card check campaign has mostly petered out.[14] The card check system avoids the need for a subsequent election once workers have expressed their pro-union preferences in writing. In principle this should prevent employers and outsiders putting undue pressure on workers to vote against union representation in an election, for example by threatening to close the plant if the workers unionize. Card check is better than the system we have now, but it is far too modest and not sufficiently democratic. Oregon's state-level card check program has yielded limited results.[15]

Card check is designed to get around the problem of political and economic coercion in representation votes by doing away with the votes. That is baby with the bathwater thinking. Workers need more freedom and democracy in the workplace, not less. Our current system is extraordinarily unfree. It prohibits workers from engaging in strikes to support workers at other firms, prohibits supervisors from joining unions along with the workers they supervise, and authorizes states to prohibit companies from agreeing closed union-only shops. Together these prohibitions represent substantial infringements on workers' rights to free association and freedom of action. They are fundamentally untenable, unfair, and un-American. Our current regulation of unions is anything but democratic.

There are many possible models for workplace democracy, but some form of workplace democracy is a progressive must-have for 2016.

Signing up for a union should be as easy as open enrollment for health and pension plans. Every year or two, all workers in all workplaces—in all states—should be given the opportunity to vote for representation. And if workers vote for representation, they should be free to take all reasonable actions that they perceive to be in their own interests. A free economy in a free society requires free workers. Everyone should have the opportunity to join a union, every year. If they did, you can bet that employers would be much more civil in their behavior toward those who make their businesses work.

9
SET A LIVING
MINIMUM WAGE

In his 2014 State of the Union address, President Barack Obama embraced the movement for a $10.10 minimum wage. Two weeks later he went even further, issuing an executive order that set $10.10 an hour as the minimum wage for all federal contractors, effective January 1, 2015. As President Obama put it in his address, this executive order requires "federal contractors to pay their federally-funded employees a fair wage of at least $10.10 an hour—because if you cook our troops' meals or wash their dishes, you shouldn't have to live in poverty."[1] This new federal contractor minimum will be indexed to inflation. The statutory minimum wage that applies to all other American employers is not indexed to inflation. As a result, its real value has declined steeply over the years.[2]

Does the President's $10.10 an hour represent a fair wage? Maybe. A living wage? Hardly. No one can really support a family on minimum wage employment, even if the minimum is raised to $10.10 an hour. At $10.10 an hour it would be difficult even to support yourself, never mind a family. And that's assuming you could find full-time work, which you probably couldn't. Very few minimum wage workers can find full-time employment, even full-time employment may not be available year-round, and all workers get sick sometimes, or have to care for sick children, or (God forbid) need a day off.

But in the end, the root problem is the low wage. The proposed $10.10 minimum isn't based on any real analysis of what it costs to live in 21st-century America. It is carefully calibrated to meet the sensitive political criterion of raising families out of poverty—very carefully calibrated indeed. The 2014 federal poverty threshold for a family of three (the standard Census Bureau reference family) is $19,790 a year.[3] The current Federal Reserve inflation target is 2% inflation per year.[4] Since the federal poverty thresholds are indexed to inflation, the anticipated poverty threshold for 2015 is $20,186 a year for a family of three. At $10.10 an hour a person working 40 hours a week, 52 weeks a year—minus 10 unpaid federal holidays—would earn $20,200 a year, or exactly $14 more than the poverty threshold. Ten dollars an hour wouldn't do it. Not even $10.09. If inflation expectations for 2015 hold firm, a full-time worker would have to make exactly $10.10 an hour, working every working day except the 10 federal holidays, to bring a family of three just over the threshold.[5]

So the magic number of $10.10 an hour will technically lift the spouse and (one) child of a full-time, year-round worker out of poverty in 2015. The poverty thresholds are indexed to inflation and the President's executive order indexes the $10.10 minimum wage for federal contractors to inflation. So from 2015, for the rest of time, no worker on a federally funded project need ever live in poverty again. Poverty problem solved.

President Obama's solution to the poverty problem is very neat, and of course there's nothing wrong with a modest raise for some of the worst-paid victims of government outsourcing. But make no mistake: It is modest. And it does not represent a living wage. More realistic living wages are available from the Living Wage Project at the Massachusetts Institute of Technology (MIT). The MIT living wage for Washington, D.C., where the employees of many federal contractors work, is $23.54 an hour for a worker supporting a family composed of two adults and a child.[6] Across the Potomac River in Arlington, Virginia it's $23.12. And in down-at-the-heels Charles Town, West Virginia it's $17.18. Just supporting yourself in Charles Town requires a full-time job paying $8.48 an hour. Better not have children.

The federal poverty line is set ridiculously low because the federal poverty thresholds were not designed for life in 21st-century America. The poverty threshold of $19,790 a year for a family of three was calibrated to supply a "subsistence" living wage for a family of three in 1963, not 2014. It was then updated until 1969 to reflect increases in food prices. Since then, it has been updated every year to reflect increases in all prices for urban consumers based on the Consumer Price Index (CPI).[7] The current official poverty thresholds thus represent the standards of living that prevailed half a century ago, and counting. It is a crazy but politically convenient idea to set a living standard in stone and leave it there without updates for half a century. Nearly 60% of the US population today weren't even alive in 1969.[8] It is difficult to imagine the United States of 1969 settling for a poverty line that was based on 1924 standards of living. Yet that is effectively what our official poverty thresholds do today.

When the federal poverty thresholds were linked to the CPI in 1969, 12.1% of Americans lived below the poverty line. In 2012 the equivalent figure was 15.0%.[9] A greater proportion of Americans live in poverty today than did 45 years ago. And to be clear: today's poverty line is a 1969 standard of poverty. Literally speaking, a greater proportion of Americans live today in what would have been considered poverty in 1969 than actually lived in poverty in 1969. It is crucially important to stress that the 1969 poverty thresholds and today's poverty thresholds are the same thresholds. They have been updated for inflation, but they have not been updated to account for any increases in living standards since the 1960s. The fact that the proportion of Americans living in 1969-style poverty is higher now than it was in 1969 is all the more shocking when you consider that real US national income per person (adjusted for inflation) has more than doubled since 1969.[10] If the poverty rate has gone up at the same time that total income per person has more than doubled, you can bet that something is wrong. That something is the minimum wage.

In 1969 the minimum wage for most private sector workers was $1.60 an hour.[11] That is equivalent to $10.24 today's money, adjusted for inflation using the CPI. That is higher than President Obama's seemingly ambitious target of $10.10 an hour for 2015. It is 41% above the actual federal minimum wage of $7.25 an hour. In other words, the President's preferred minimum wage of $10.10 an hour would come close to restoring the minimum wage that prevailed in 1969, adjusted for inflation. More reasonable approaches to updating the 1969 minimum wage to contemporary standards are available. If the minimum wage had grown in lockstep with growth in national income per person since 1969, it would have reached $16.88 an hour in 2013.[12] Assuming that GDP per capita continues to grow at a modest 2.5% per year in 2014 and 2015, the equivalent figure for 2015 would be a minimum wage of $17.73 an hour, or 145% above the current statutory minimum wage. That's quite a bit higher than President Obama's proposed increase to $10.10.

The $17.73 an hour figure is not some kind of socialist dream number pulled from thin air. It is the minimum wage that the United States would have today if Congress had chosen to index the minimum wage to overall economic growth. And a $17.73 an hour minimum wage would be a living wage for the 2010s. In fact, it is almost exactly equal to the $15 living wage demanded by the 2012-13 fast food industry protesters once you add in 10 paid sick days, 10 paid vacation days, and 10 paid holidays. The 2012-13 fast food protests were coordinated by community groups like Fast Food Forward in New York and Fight for 15 in Chicago, with support from the Service Employees International Union and other pro-worker organizations. The voters of tiny SeaTac, Washington (home of Seattle-Tacoma International Airport) led the country in passing a $15 minimum wage law that took effect on January 1, 2014.[13] On June 2, 2014 SeaTac's much larger neighbor Seattle followed suit.[14] Seattle's new $15 minimum wage has been challenged in the courts on the basis of its distinction between large and small employers, but in the meantime higher wages are due to be phased in starting in April, 2015.[15]

Unfortunately, the new SeaTac and Seattle minimum wages are only indexed to inflation, so they will slowly deteriorate over time just as the federal poverty thresholds have. As a result, progressives in Washington state will eventually have to fight these battles all over again. Nonetheless, Washington is clearly leading the country. No jurisdiction outside the state of Washington has mandated a $15 living wage, but the current situation is not all gloom and doom. In line with President Obama's plea to increase the minimum wage for all workers, Connecticut and Maryland have raised their minimum wages to $10.10 an hour, effective in 2017 and 2018, respectively. California is due for an increase to $10.00 an hour in 2016. All told, 20 states currently have minimum wages that are higher than the nationwide federal minimum of $7.25 an hour.[16] Many cities also have minimum wage laws, including San Francisco ($10.74, indexed to inflation), Santa Fe ($10.66, indexed to inflation), and Washington, D.C. ($8.25, rising to $11.50 in 2016).

Meanwhile the federal minimum wage remains firmly stuck in the mud at $7.25 an hour, the President's executive order raising the minimum to $10.10 an hour in 2015 only applies to federal contractors, and no one believes that a living minimum wage of $15.00 an hour is politically realistic anywhere outside of Washington state. Even New York, under progressive mayor Bill de Blasio, has only followed President Obama's example of raising wages for employees of government contractors.[17] Under New York state law the city cannot currently set its own statutory minimum wages, though this may change in the near future.[18]

Politics aside, the $7.25 minimum wage is a national disgrace, and even $10.10 an hour is inadequate to carry the "progressive" label. Progressive policies must do more than restore gains made in the last century and since lost. That's not "progress." Progressive policies must move our country forward toward liberty and justice for all, and that includes low-wage workers. There is no liberty in the freedom to be exploited, and there is no justice in exploitation. There is no law of economics that says that the market wage must be a living wage. But a democratic society can and should have laws that are higher and nobler than the laws of economics.

Twenty years before Barack Obama was even born, an earlier President giving an earlier State of the Union address looked "forward to a world founded upon four essential human freedoms": freedom of speech, freedom of worship, freedom from want, and freedom from fear."[19] President Franklin Roosevelt died 70 years ago. He did more than any other President to save American freedoms from the twin threats of depression and dictatorship. He maintained that the Four Freedoms were "no vision of a distant millennium" but a "definite basis for a kind of world attainable in our own time and generation."

Roosevelt's two "freedoms of " we have. They are liberties that we all take for granted. No politician, conservative or progressive, would ever question Americans' freedom of speech and freedom of worship.

Roosevelt's two "freedoms from" we still lack. They are calls for justice that have gone completely unheeded for the last 40 years. And a living wage is the cornerstone of both freedom from want and freedom from fear.

The "distant millennium" of which Roosevelt spoke has come and gone, and many Americans still live in want of a decent income and in fear of losing their low-wage jobs. President Obama's call for a $10.10 minimum wage is better than nothing, but better than nothing is not progress. A living wage for all—that would be progress. And if President Obama can get us to $10.10 an hour, the next President should forget about indexing it to inflation. A minimum wage indexed to inflation would mean a 1969 poverty wage for the rest of eternity. A living wage means a minimum wage that rises to meet the higher living standards of each new generation. It must be a living threshold, not a dead hand of the past freezing real wages for all eternity. The progressive agenda should include a truly living minimum wage benchmarked not to 1969 or 2016 but to our hopes for a brighter future still to come.

10
UPGRADE TO
10-10-10

Far and away the most memorable slogan of the 2012 election campaign was the Republican candidate Herman Cain's "9-9-9" plan. It sure beats "Forward" (Barack Obama) and "Believe in America" (Mitt Romney) and is right up there with "Commerce, Education and the... uh, what's the third one there?" (Rick Perry).[1] Herman Cain and his economic advisor, Cleveland accountant Rich Lowrie, called for a 9% value added tax, a 9% flat income tax, and 9% federal sales tax to replace all existing federal taxes.[2] It has been suggested Cain's campaign copied the 9-9-9 plan from the default tax structure implemented in the computer game *Sim City*.[3] Whether or not this is true, no one believes that 9-9-9 is a practical solution to the problems of contemporary society. No one, that is, outside the Herman Cain campaign team and presumably the still-operating 9-9-9 Fund political action committee.[4]

After dropping out of the Republican nomination battle, Cain was invited to deliver the Tea Party State of the Union response in January 2012. Look for a return of the 9-9-9 plan in 2016, with or without Herman Cain.[5] It might raise taxes on nearly all American households while still somehow managing to decimate overall federal government revenues, but there's no denying that it's a great slogan.[6] Even if Cain doesn't run in 2016, expect someone else to pick it up.

Whether or not Cain makes a comeback in 2016, progressives would do well to up the ante one notch by introducing their own 10-10-10 plan. The 10-10-10 plan would require all employers to provide 10 paid sick days, 10 paid holidays, and 10 paid vacation days a year for all full-time workers, prorated for part-time workers as well. Those with well-paid professional jobs may not realize that other people don't already have 10-10-10, but they don't. Far from it. For many working Americans, 10-10-10 would be a dream come true.

Take sick days. Today just 65%—less than two-thirds—of all American workers have any opportunity to take paid sick days at all, according to official government statistics. This figure covers all workers, both full- and part-time. Hispanic Americans are particularly disadvantaged when it comes to sick leave.[7] Many people expect paid sick days to be an ordinary benefit of a full-time job, but only 74% of full-time private sector workers receive any paid sick days at all.[8] For part-time workers the figures are catastrophic: just 26 % of all workers and 24 % of private sector workers have the opportunity to take paid sick days. And part-time employment is the fastest-growing segment of the labor force.

The real situation for vulnerable parts of the workforce is even worse than these statistics indicate. Government statistics completely ignore the cash economy of illegal and semi-legal employment. Day laborers who wait before dawn in the parking lots of home improvement warehouses every morning looking for work do not get paid sick days—and they are not included in government employment benefits surveys. Accounting for those who fall between the cracks of government record-keeping and those who technically get paid sick days but are afraid to use them, it is likely that slightly less than half of all American workers can feel secure about calling in sick when they come down with the flu, without fear of losing pay—or even their jobs. Fewer still can afford to get seriously ill, be involved in a car crash, or need an operation.

You should at least be able to get sick on a holiday. The United States has 10 federal holidays: New Year's Day, Martin Luther King Day, Presidents' Day, Memorial Day, Independence Day, Labor Day, Columbus Day, Veterans' Day, Thanksgiving, and Christmas. Except of course that in the United States your employer doesn't have to give you a paid day off just because it's a public holiday. Only 76% of American workers get any paid holidays at all. Among part-timers that figure drops to 38%.

Similarly, paid vacation days are the preserve of well-paid full-time workers. Among all workers the proportion receiving paid vacation time is 74%. Among part-timers it is 34%. State and local governments are particularly stingy with paid vacation time. Only two thirds of full-time state and local government workers receive paid vacation days.

All of these figures get worse the farther you go down the pay scale, and all of them are worse for small employers. In the bottom quarter of the economy (those paid at or near minimum wage) only 30% of private sector workers get any paid sick days and slightly less than half get paid holidays and vacation days. And again, these figures apply only to the kinds of employers that get caught up in federal statistical surveys. Your local supermarket is in. Your local unregistered after-hours parking lot cleaning company is almost certainly out.

And that is part of the problem. Big companies now outsource many services that used to be performed by their own employees. The result is that a job with a barely regulated big business has been turned into a job with a completely unregulated small business. Among large private-sector employers of 500 or more workers, 81% offer their workers paid sick days. Among small employers of fewer than 100 employees, the figure is 51%. When jobs are outsourced from big companies to small contractors, benefits like sick pay tend to disappear. The lack of benefits and poor working conditions are the reasons why small private contractors can clean parking lots, mow lawns, and unload trucks more cheaply than big, super-efficient retailers can do these jobs for themselves.

For example, industry bulletin boards report that Walmart pays its contractors and through them its sub-contractors anywhere from $22 to $50 to clean an entire store parking lot in the middle of the night.[9] These rates seem to be typical for other big-box retail stores as well. To put these rates into perspective, a big box retail store can have its parking lot cleaned overnight so that it is litter-free and ready to welcome your car in the morning for roughly the price of a nice shirt. Think how many shirts (toasters, drills) these stores sell in a day and it gives you some idea what a trivial expense cleaning is for a large store. Despite these already super-low rates, industry bulletin boards are full of online posts from contractors complaining about being screwed down from $35 to $30 to $25 a job. Big retailers are always looking for that extra $5. Mind you, that's not an extra $5 per customer or $5 per item sold. That's an extra $5 a day—or a store the size of a Walmart. No one ever got rich throwing away pennies.

In this business-outsourcing sector of the economy if you don't work, you don't get paid. It's as simple as that. And the big businesses that do the outsourcing typically shirk any responsibility for what happens to the outsourced workers, including injuries. Don't even ask about retirement. But then, what's wrong with paying people only for the hours they actually work? Many high-skill professionals work on this principle. Just ask any freelance writer, designer, or architect. Or any small business owner. Freelancers and small business owners have to set aside savings for rainy days all on their own. No one gives them paid sick days, holidays, or vacation days. They rely on their own discipline and planning to pay for time off.

The difference between freelancers and hourly workers is that at the federal minimum wage of $7.25 an hour, or even at President Obama's preferred minimum wage of $10.10 an hour, it is nearly impossible to save for a rainy day. A bare minimum 10-10-10 benefits plan of 10 paid sick days, 10 paid holidays, and 10 paid vacation days a year amounts to 30 days off out of a typical 260-day work year. Roughly speaking, workers have to save 11.5% of their take-home pay every week to fund a 10-10-10 plan through personal discipline and planning alone. Personal discipline is quite a tall order when your total take-home pay is just $268 a week (minimum wage minus payroll taxes) or even $373 a week ($10.10 an hour minus payroll taxes). Planning can be even harder. People who have irregular, poorly paid jobs with no benefits tend to know many other people who have irregular, poorly paid jobs with no benefits. When people do somehow manage to save for a rainy day, more often than not they find themselves saving for someone else's rainy day. That is to say, if it comes to a choice between keeping your savings intact or paying your son's speeding ticket to keep him out of jail, it takes a hard heart to save your savings for your own rainy day.

Research on micro-savings plans confirms this. In 2011 and 2012, low- and middle-income Americans in four cities were recruited for a pilot study on the impact of incentives to save.[10] Participants were offered a 50% bonus (up to $500) if they saved up to $1,000 of their tax refunds for at least one year. Depending on how the results are interpreted, between one quarter and one third of the study participants were unable to keep their pledged savings in the bank for a full year, despite the massive reward of a 50% bonus at the end of the study period. And this study represents a best case scenario: Research subjects got their money in a lump sum (through their tax refunds) instead of having to save money a few dollars a week out of their paychecks. In addition, many of the participants were nowhere near poor (enrollees had taxable incomes of up to $50,000). Even among those who saved for a full year and got their 50% bonuses, more than 60% cashed out and withdrew all their savings immediately after the end of the one-year lock-up period. If people find it difficult to save small sums under such favorable conditions, it is simply unrealistic to expect low-wage workers to save up for their own sick days, holidays, and vacation days.

The progressive solution to the rainy day problem is a federally mandated 10-10-10 plan for all American workers. Most Americans already have at least 10 sick days, 10 holidays, and 10 vacation days. Most Americans take basic benefits like this for granted and consider 10-10-10 (or better) a basic benefit that defines a "real" job. Well, sweeping parking lots, mowing lawns, and unloading trucks for minimum wage (or less) are real jobs too, and Americans who take on these tough tasks rarely get 10-10-10. They are lucky to get any days off at all. Whether working in air-conditioned offices or on sun-baked parking lots, all progressives can agree that 10-10-10 is a basic minimum standard that no one should have to go without. The demand for 10-10-10 should be the rallying cry that unites us all. Everyone needs 10-10-10.

Herman Cain etched 9-9-9 permanently into America's collective political memory. For a while it made him the Republican front-runner in the 2012 primary campaign. In 2016 progressives should do him one better. One, one, and one better. Every progressive Presidential candidate should embrace 10-10-10 from the very start of the 2016 primary season. It is hard to imagine a progressive argument against it. Who doesn't deserve 10-10-10? Everyone deserves a break now and then, and even people who don't deserve a break still need one. The 10-10-10 plan ensures that everyone gets the time off that everyone needs. It's the least we can do—and we should do it. Say it often and say it loud: 10-10-10 in 2016!

11
PUT AN END TO THE PRISON STATE

On any given day nearly seven million adult Americans are under the supervision of the nation's criminal justice system: in prison, on probation, or on parole.[1]

That is more than 2% of the entire population and nearly 3% of the adult population. If the prison system were a state, it would be the 14th largest, just behind Washington and well ahead of Massachusetts. It would make an average-sized country, much bigger than Libya but slightly smaller than Serbia. The United States imprisonment rate is more twice that of any other country in the Organisation for Economic Co-operation and Development (OECD), more than four times that of any country in western Europe, and more than five times the rich-country average.[2] It is 12 times the rate in Japan. Simply put, the United States imprisons a larger proportion of its population than any other country in the world.[3] It also has the highest total number of prisoners of any country in the world, except perhaps China (where prison statistics are not fully transparent). Over 20% of all the world's prisoners are locked up in American prisons. In short, the land of the free is the home of the jailed.

Drill down and the numbers get even worse, particularly for men (though the number of women prisoners is rising fast).[4] More than 5% of all adult American men are currently under the supervision of the criminal justice system. Men make up over 90% of all prisoners, nearly 90% of people on parole, and about 75% of people on probation. Put these figures together and it turns out that about 1.3% of all American men are hidden behind bars at any given time.[5] Among African-American men age 25-39 this figure rises to more than 6% in jail at any one time.[6] The proportion of African-American men who spend at least some part of their lives in jail is presumably much higher, probably around one quarter, though this is difficult to calculate accurately and widely cited figures may be suspect.

Once you've been arrested or sent to jail, life gets much harder in many ways, whether or not you were actually convicted of a crime. Obviously, most employers prefer not to employ ex-convicts, most landlords prefer not to rent to ex-convicts, and most people prefer not to marry ex-convicts. In the words of prison reform activist Maya Schenwar: "Housing, food, health care, and the heavy labor of emotional readjustment can loom as insurmountable obstacles."[7] Few studies have been done of the life chances of ex-convicts, but one major study found that the median monthly income for ex-convicts was just $410 two months after release and $700 eight months after release.[8] Fewer than half of the ex-convicts in this study had been able to find legal employment. Unsurprisingly, a systematic review of the academic literature confirms that imprisonment has "far-reaching" impacts on education, jobs, and life in general.[9] Experience as a convict can even be an impediment to getting a job as a criminologist.[10]

Even for those who have never been convicted of a crime, or who have been unambiguously cleared of committing crimes, merely being arrested or named as a "person of interest" in an investigation can ruin their lives and careers. The Department of Justice admitted as much when in 2008 it agreed to pay the former government scientist named as a "person of interest" in the 2001 anthrax terrorism investigation a multi-million dollar settlement.[11] That person will not be named here, but of course the damage has been done. In the internet age every small-town police blotter is permanently and conveniently searchable for the rest of eternity. Nothing is forgotten. The European Union has recognized this as a problem and introduced a newfound "right to be forgotten" into its human rights rules, but there is no chance of this right being extended to Americans.[12]

Now a new, highly motivated pressure group has been born in the United States to promote mass incarceration—the private prisons industry.[13] According to a major report from the American Civil Liberties Union (ACLU), in 2010, "the two largest private prison companies alone received nearly $3 billion dollars in revenue, and their top executives, according to one source, each received annual compensation packages worth well over $3 million."[14] This newfound revenue stream has been associated with massive levels of spending on lobbying and political campaign contributions at all levels of government.[15] Official statistics show that 8.7% of all prisoners and 18.6% of federal prisoners are held in private prisons.[16] Now that the genie is out of the bottle, industry lobbying will ensure that these numbers only go up.

This is no way to run a country. Too many people are in prison for too long, and too many people are in prison for crimes they did not commit or for activities that should never have been classified as crimes in the first place.

The good news is that the prison state is now officially in decline. A recent government report found that "1 in every 35 adult residents in the United States was under some form of correctional supervision at yearend 2012, the lowest rate observed since 1997."[17] New incarcerations are down too. In 2012 an estimated 444,591 people were newly committed to prison by the nation's courts, down from nearly half a million in 2006—a drop of about 10%. The bad news is that these declines are only occurring because states can no longer afford their bloated prison systems. Most of the decline has occurred in California, where the state's Public Safety Realignment policy simply diverted nonviolent criminals from state prisons to local jails and parole offices.

Even the lower flow of new inmates to prisons in 2012 was three times as high as the number of people who were sent to prison each year in the 1970s.[18] The 1970s was the decade of the angry young man. Now we warehouse angry young men until they become cantankerous but harmless old men. Crime rates have come down dramatically since the 1970s, though it is not clear that this decline is due to mass incarceration. Scientific opinion varies widely on this. After all, people are usually imprisoned after they commit murder, not before. In any case most prisoners are imprisoned for far more prosaic crimes than murder. Some 70% of new admissions to state prisons and the vast majority of new admissions to federal prisons are for nonviolent crimes.[19] No one is suggesting probation for murder or rape, but imprisonment may not be the best way to deal with identity theft or cocaine possession.

Or protesting. One of the most unsavory aspects of the American criminal justice system is its penchant for locking people up if they exhibit anything but complete and utter submission to the will of the police. Many Occupy Wall Street protesters experienced this kind of treatment firsthand. Often minority young people experience much worse treatment. The Trayvon Martin shooting in Florida and the Michael Brown shooting in Missouri are two of the most tragic examples of violence used by police officers and security guards against young, unarmed, mostly African-American suspects. No one knows for sure whether or not these examples amount to a trend because the government does not keep statistics on the number of people it kills accidentally. The government does, however, keep detailed statistics on the number of people it kills on purpose.

Between 1930 and 2011 a grand total of 5,296 people were executed by federal and state governments, including military executions. For 10 years in the middle of that period (1967-76) there were no executions at all. From the time executions resumed in 1977 through 2011 there have been 1,277 executions, or about 35-40 per year.[20] The number of people whose convictions or sentences have been overturned since the end of the moratorium on executions? 3,059. Since 1977, more than twice as many people on death row have been exonerated as have been executed.[21] In fact, more than one third of all people sentenced to death by American governments since 1973 have been exonerated—so far. Since it takes years of legal appeals to have a sentence overturned, the lifetime exoneration rate is well over 50%. Considering how difficult it is to overturn a wrongful conviction, the true innocence rate is presumably even higher.

Federal and state governments continue to execute people at a rate of about 40 per year.[22] Considering that there are about 16,000 murders committed every year in the United States and that about half of the people sentenced to death are probably innocent of the specific murders for which they have been convicted, it is difficult to see any good reason for continuing the death penalty lottery.[23] The death penalty may or may not be immoral. It may or may not be effective. But it is obviously and unquestionably ridiculous from a criminal justice standpoint.

Where the death penalty makes sense is as the ultimate symbol of social control, of the police state. A government that has the power of life and death over its citizens is a powerful government indeed. Too powerful, as both progressives and conservative can agree. It doesn't take a conspiracy theorist to see that American governments of all levels—from small town sheriffs to the Department of Homeland Security—now have too much raw, physical power over our bodies and our lives. They push us around too much. All of us.

The National Employment Law Project estimates that 27.8% of the adult population, or about 65 million people, have criminal records that would show up in a routine employment check.[24] This implies that for an individual person the lifetime probability of accumulating a criminal record is well over one third. Many of those criminal records may be well deserved. But as a country are we really that bad? Or are our governments abusing their powers to arrest, prosecute, incarcerate, and even kill us in the name of justice?

Our governments at all levels certainly seem to be arming themselves for some kind of Syria-style internal war. In March 2012 a police aerial surveillance drone in suburban Montgomery County, Texas crashed into the county's SWAT team and smashed a headlight on its armored personnel carrier. Amusing as this incident was, it should have raised three important questions. Why does a suburban county of 500,000 people need an observation drone? Why does a suburban county of

500,000 people need an armored personnel carrier? And why does a suburban county of 500,000 people even need a SWAT team? We're talking about suburban Houston, not suburban Damascus.

Our governments want drones, tanks, and SWAT teams for the same reason they want the death penalty: to keep us under control. Despite his background in Constitutional law and his personal background growing up black and male in America, President Obama has embraced and expanded the police state that makes social control possible. His successor should change course before private prison corporations become the next military industrial complex and local law enforcement agencies become the next CIA. It is probably too late for a pacifist President to shut down the Pentagon. But it is not too late for a progressive President to change the culture of law enforcement in America. It should be easy to cut the domestic drone-and-APC budget in a time of austerity. And the next President can renationalize the federal prison system by making the terms of prison contracts unattractive to private sector firms.

In April 2014 Montgomery County crashed another surveillance drone, this time into a lake. The United States may have a very effective military, but Americans are not very good at running a prison state. We're lucky about that, but we shouldn't push our luck. Progressives, conservatives, and all sensible people should come together in 2016 to demand that all candidates for President agree to run the country on a purely civilian basis. Modern governments have at their disposal awesome powers of domination and control. We have to make sure that our federal, state, and local governments don't use those powers to dominate and control us.

12
PASS A NATIONAL ABORTION LAW

There are no easy answers in the abortion debate. Passions run high, and with good reason. But wherever you stand in the abortion debate, one thing seems clear. America needs one law on abortion, not 50 state laws or 500 local laws. Abortion has been more or less legal in the United States since 1973, but it is more legal in some states and places than in others. Is abortion legal if women are harassed going into and coming out of abortion clinics? Is abortion legal if a woman has to travel to another county or state to find a doctor who will see her? Is abortion legal if safe, quality abortion care is not available at all? Whatever the balance between a woman's right to an abortion and society's interest in her fetus should not depend on where a woman happens to live, work, or seek health care. Localism in government administration is a fine principle, but localism in official morality is not. One nation indivisible must have a policy on abortion that can accommodate 300 million or more different opinions without trampling on the rights and needs of women, their fetuses, and their families.

National abortion law currently rests on the Constitution as interpreted by a series of Supreme Court decisions, most famously the 1973 Roe v. Wade decision that legalized abortion nationwide.[1] The Constitutional basis for the right to abortion found in Roe v. Wade is built on the thin reed of the 14th Amendment, passed in 1868 to prevent states from reintroducing new forms of slavery. The 14th Amendment stipulates that no state shall "deprive any person of life, liberty, or property, without due process of law," from which has been implied a general right to privacy, from which has been implied a right to privacy in pregnancy, from which has been implied a right to abortion. This is good so far as it goes, but it is hardly a secure footing on which to base such a basic human right as reproductive self-determination.

The problem is: If we had a national abortion law, what would it be? For most of the last 40 years the mood in Congress has been decidedly reactionary. Congress has been much more disposed to restrict abortion rights than to protect them.[2] Are the Members of Congress really so anti-abortion, or does Congress act irresponsibly because individual Members can rest easy in the knowledge that if any of their loved ones ever needed an abortion she could just go to another state, or even overseas if necessary? Only the Members of Congress know for sure. Besides, having a daughter who needs an abortion is something different from needing one oneself. Very few serving Members of Congress are of an age and gender that they are likely to be put in the position of needing discreet abortion care.

What if there were no Roe v. Wade to serve as a backstop for a spineless Congress that is unwilling to face the need for the federal legislation of abortion rights? What would Congress do if abortion became illegal in most or all of the United States? We may not have to wait very long to find out. According to research from the Guttmacher Institute, 46 states allow medical professionals to personally refuse to participate in an abortion, 43 states allow healthcare institutions to refuse to perform abortions, 42 states prohibit abortions after a certain gestational age, 19 states ban use of the dilation and extraction abortion procedure (pejoratively labeled "partial-birth" abortion), and 9 states even restrict private companies from providing abortion coverage in insurance policies (so much for the free market).[3] State discouragement of abortion, state pressure on abortion providers, and state encouragement of anti-abortion medical professionals are all forces that tend to reduce the availability of safe abortion services. Research from the Huffington Post shows that 11 states saw reductions in abortion availability of more than 20% over the brief period 2010-13, including Texas and Pennsylvania. All in all the availability of abortion care declined in 17 states. Only two states saw expanded access.[4]

A major driver of this decline in the availability of abortion care is the so-called TRAP strategy: targeted regulation of abortion providers.

These are politically motivated state rules that impose frivolous burdens on healthcare providers with the obvious intention of discouraging them from offering abortion services. State TRAP rules include new regulations on things like clinic room size and corridor width that specifically target abortion providers but not other, similar healthcare organizations. Many TRAP rules sound eminently reasonable on the surface and seem designed to protect patient health. For example, the Guttmacher Institute reports that 15 states mandate that abortion providers have relationships with local hospitals, presumably in order to deal with unlikely but possibly dangerous complications resulting from abortion.[5] The truth behind these rules is revealed by the fact that the 15 states that have passed them are a rogue's gallery of mainly southern and midwestern states that in general show little concern for maternal health except when it comes to restricting access to abortion.

Then there are the cruel rituals imposed on women seeking an abortion: forced adoption counseling, forced information (often misinformation) about fetal pain, and most nefarious of all forced viewing of ultrasound images of fetuses. All of these are transparently intended to cause discomfort in the patient, not to improve maternal health. States are also complicit in allowing the exposure of pregnant women to harsh treatment at the hands of violent anti-abortion activists.[6] When anti-abortion activists are willing to harass, intimidate, or even kill to make their point, it is not surprising that many institutions think twice about providing abortion care. This fact was violently imposed on the nation's attention on May 31, 2009 when abortion provider Dr. George Tiller was murdered while handing out church bulletins by a crazed anti-abortion activist, the fourth doctor in the last 20 years to be killed for performing abortions.[7]

Tiller had long been a bête noire of the extremist anti-abortion pressure group Operation Rescue. For example, an undated fundraising letter from Operation Rescue reads "WE TOOK PICTURES [links to 15 hidden-camera-style photos of pregnant women] of the very-pregnant young mothers as they were going into Tiller's killing center, one after another, *to have their babies killed* [emphasis in original].[8] Operation Rescue boasts on its website that the number of clinics that provide abortion services has fallen from 2,176 in 1991 to just 582 in 2013.[9] Most of the remaining clinics are concentrated in a small number of states, and nearly one third of them are operated by a single organization, Planned Parenthood. It is amazing that any medical professionals are willing to risk their lives to provide abortion services. They certainly shouldn't have to.

America's state governments have amply demonstrated through both commission and omission that they cannot be trusted to responsibly and dispassionately regulate abortion care. Clearly, some form of federal intervention is necessary. Progressives must accept that this intervention must inevitably include some degree of regulation. Abortion is a medical procedure akin to minor surgery, not a personal lifestyle choice like wearing a condom or taking the pill. And there is the very real matter of the fetus. Women's health activists tend to leave the fetus out of the picture because it's bad press for abortion rights. But no pragmatic policy debate on access to abortion services can ignore the fact that a human fetus is involved.

Earlier in pregnancy, at the embryo stage, society's (and thus government's) interest in the developing pregnancy is less clear-cut. Anti-abortion fundamentalists who argue that life begins at conception are easy to ridicule. Should we give social security numbers to embryos that fail to implant in the uterus? Should we imprison women if they create embryos through in vitro fertilization that they do not later implant for pregnancy? The conservative embryo "personhood" movement seeks just these kinds of outcomes. Personhood activists seek to define every fertilized egg as a human being. This is the lunatic fringe of the anti-abortion movement, albeit a lunatic fringe with a large presence in many state legislatures.

Once the process of pregnancy has moved from embryo to implantation to fetus, the shoe is on the other foot. Free abortion on demand at all times in all cases is not a viable policy position in a highly bureaucratic, pluralistic society like our own. Human decency, the interests of society, and sometimes plain administrative necessity really do sometimes outweigh a woman's right to control over her own body. Just as no sane person would imprison a woman for failing to implant a frozen embryo, no sane person would equate killing a baby moments before birth with excising an unwanted mole. And in fact no sane person really does take this position. So sane people should stop talking about absolute, unlimited human rights to abortion.

In all sorts of made-up scenarios about abortion rights and responsibilities sane people repeatedly come up with one answer: "it depends." And if "it depends," then we're not talking about absolute issues that involve the very definition of human life. We're talking about public policies that involve difficult choices that no one wants to have to make. The answers to all questions about women's rights over their bodies and society's responsibilities toward embryos, fetuses, and babies comes down to situational "it depends" answers, and in every case it depends on a lot of things. That should be the motto for the whole abortion debate—it depends.

And because it depends on so many things, abortion is a difficult decision best left to women and their healthcare providers, with a strong assumption of trust toward the pregnant woman and a strong assumption of professionalism on the part of healthcare providers. Neither pregnant women nor healthcare providers are in the killing business. In general they should be trusted to do the right thing for themselves, for their families, and for society. That said, government does have an appropriate role to play in the regulation of abortion and in the setting of general guidelines for medical professionals who are involved in providing abortion services. The regulation of medical professions is ordinarily a state-level function, but if state governments cannot responsibly play this role with regard to abortion then the federal government should step in. In legislating on abortion, Congress should stay away from defining "life" or counting gestational weeks. Instead it should step in to ensure that women in all parts of the United States have access to safe, affordable abortion services. It should also define the areas over which states can exercise reasonable local discretion in the regulation of abortion.

We all know that Congress will never tackle such a tough issue on its own. The next President will have to prod Congress into action. A President who is the President of all 50 states is in a stronger position than is any particular Member of Congress to push Congress toward settling a compromise that works for all 50 states. It won't be easy, but it is doable, and it is necessary. The key to progress on this issue is for the President to get Congress to debate a national abortion policy, a legislative replacement for Roe v. Wade, instead of focusing on piecemeal abortion-related legislation. The only existing federal law on abortion is the Bush-era Partial-Birth Abortion Ban Act of 2003 that prohibits the dilation and extraction method of abortion. This is a national embarrassment and a poor model for future legislation. The gory details of medical procedures are surely a matter for doctors to decide, not lawyers.

A progressive President should shift the terms of the abortion debate as only a President can. The overwhelming majority of Americans— around 80%—believe that abortion should be legal, depending on the circumstances.[10] An outspoken President with strong moral convictions can leverage that 80% popular approval into meaningful political gains. The federalization of abortion rights will take moral conviction, hard work, and a willingness on the part of progressives to accept a compromise position that incorporates some restrictions and reservations. Clearly the states cannot be trusted to arrive at such a compromise. If a progressive President can convince Congress to show some common sense, perhaps the federal government can.

13
LET PEOPLE VOTE

The United States is the world's oldest continuously operating democracy, with an unbroken history of national elections going back to 1788. Individual American states and cities can trace their democratic traditions back to the 1600s. The United States can rightfully and proudly call itself the birthplace of modern democracy. No other country comes close. American democracy may not be perfect, but for the first 200 years of the republic the overall trend was unambiguously toward perfection. Progress went in fits and starts, but it always went forward. Between 1860 and 1945 America even went to war for freedom and democracy in the Civil War, World War I, World War II, and several smaller wars. Both at home and abroad hundreds of thousands of Americans made the ultimate sacrifice to ensure (in Abraham Lincoln's words) "that government of the people, by the people, for the people, shall not perish from the Earth."

Five years after Lincoln's Gettysburg Address the 15th Amendment to the Constitution made it illegal to prevent people from voting based on race or color. In 1919 the 19th Amendment made it illegal to prevent people from voting based on sex, and in 1962 the 24th Amendment made it illegal to prevent people from voting based on the nonpayment of taxes. In 1965 the Voting Rights Act reinforced these Constitutional protections by outlawing literacy tests and other discriminatory practices that might prevent people from voting. In 1990 the Americans with Disabilities Act expanded voting even further by mandating accommodations for people with disabilities. All told that's more than 120 years of expanding the franchise and ensuring that everyone who wants to vote is able to vote.

Despite this proud history of ever-improving democracy, in the 2012 Presidential election only 58% of the eligible population voted.

Congressional elections never even reach 50% turnout. In local elections turnout is almost always less than 10%. Most law-abiding Americans are guaranteed the right to vote, but most Americans don't vote most of the time. In a free society of course that's their choice to make. Or is it? It's one thing to chose to vote when voting is as easy as clicking on a link or mailing back a postage-paid form. It's another thing to chose to vote when voting means waiting outdoors in a six-hour line without food or water on a work day when you could lose your job if you are late to work. It can also be difficult to vote if you don't even know that an election is occurring. You can't expect people to drop by their local polling places now and then "just in case."

The first two centuries of American democracy saw repeated electoral reforms aimed at fulfilling the Constitution's promise of a more perfect Union by expanding the franchise and making it easier for people to vote. But since 1991 the historical record has been more uneven, and in many states the trend is now in the wrong direction. Many states are making it harder to vote and erecting barriers to voter registration. Voter suppression has reemerged as a dangerous strategy for winning elections. In the four years 2010-14 at least 22 states introduced new restrictions on voting, according to a report from New York University's Brennan Center for Justice.[1] These include new restrictive regulations on voter registration drives, new limitations on early voting, and new avenues for partisan lawyers to challenge voters inside polling places on election day. Far from encouraging people to vote, these measures encourage people not to bother. Even when they don't absolutely prevent people from voting, they certainly don't send the right message.

Some of the most underhanded and pernicious approaches to voter suppression involve voter ID laws. On the surface these laws sound reasonable enough: People should have to show a valid ID in order to vote. In practice in a free country like America these laws are highly repressive. After all, the United States is not (yet) a police state. In an authoritarian police state the government always knows who you are and where you live. The government can make sure that everyone always has an up-to-date ID card. If your "papers" aren't in order you can be detained, imprisoned—or worse. By contrast in a free country like the United States people are always on the move. People get married, get divorced, and change their names just because they feel like it. Teenagers go away to college without asking their parents' permission, never mind the government's. You can choose to be footloose, and you can even choose to be homeless. As a result, when you show up to vote you may have an ID card that has expired, has your old address on it, or has your old name on it. You may not have any ID card at all. In a free country you don't have to carry your "papers" to prove who you are. And in a free country that is also a democracy, you are guaranteed the right to vote.

In theory voter ID laws exist to protect the right to vote by guarding against voter impersonation. Impersonating a voter by pretending to be someone else and voting in their place is a serious crime, but it is a crime that almost never occurs. The reason is obvious: Any one vote is almost always irrelevant in a typical election. It would take massive levels of voter impersonation to swing the typical election. Studies of voter impersonation show that this simply does not happen in the United States of America. For example, an exhaustive News21 investigation was able to identify just 10 cases of in-person voter fraud occurring over the 11-year period 2000-10, or less than one per year.[3] That's one case of in-person voter impersonation per year in a country of nearly 150 million registered voters. In fact, News21 found that the most common type of voter fraud is absentee ballot fraud, which is almost 50 times as common as in-person voter fraud. But voter ID laws do nothing to protect against absentee ballot fraud.

In reality, voter ID laws exist to prevent certain types of people from voting: women (whose names change regularly), the young (whose addresses change regularly), the elderly (who often don't have drivers' licenses), and the homeless (who don't have fixed addresses).[2] To be effective in swinging an election, a voter ID law doesn't have to prevent every woman, young person, old person, and homeless person from voting. It just has to reduce voting in these categories in ways that systematically affect the total vote. Voter ID laws can suppress the vote even when people do have proper, current identification because they foster an atmosphere of fear on election day. It can be scary when partisan lawyers in suits and dark sunglasses invade your polling place and demand to see your papers. And that's what the lawyers are there for: to scare people away. They particularly try to scare away minority voters, and they succeed.[3] In a highly sophisticated study of voter ID and similar legislation, University of Maryland academics Keith Bentele and Erin O'Brien find "a very substantial and significant association between the racial composition of a state's residents or active electorate and both the proposal and passage of voter restriction legislation" that "is robust across multiple modeling approaches and controlling for a wide variety of relevant factors."[4]

Long lines are another tool used to discourage voting, especially voting by African Americans and other minorities. Massive lines for voting are almost exclusively experienced by minorities. Research by MIT political scientist Charles Stewart III shows that in the 2012 elections the residents of 75% minority zip codes waited more than twice as long to vote as the residents of 75% white zip codes.[5] There was almost no difference in waiting time by average income level. The zip codes with the longest lines were minority zip codes, not poor zip codes. Cue up pictures from Miami and Cleveland.

These kinds of problems really are serious enough to swing elections. If the 2000 Presidential election was stolen, it was stolen not by the Supreme Court and "hanging chads" but by systematic voter suppression among minorities, the elderly, the young, and the poor.[6] Hanging chads only became an issue because the actual vote was so close. In the absence of systematic voter suppression, the actual vote might not have been close at all. In its official report on the 2000 election in Florida, the United States Commission on Civil Rights was unequivocal on this point.[7] Among its conclusions:

> **The Commission's findings make one thing clear: widespread voter disenfranchisement—not the dead-heat contest—was the extraordinary feature in the Florida election."**
>
> **"Statistical data, reinforced by credible anecdotal evidence, point to the widespread denial of voting rights."**
>
> **"The disenfranchisement of Florida's voters fell most harshly on the shoulders of black voters."**

Similarly, the outcome of the 2004 Presidential election was almost certainly affected by voter suppression (if not outright fraud).[8] Lines of four hours were commonplace in minority districts in Ohio, discouraging tens of thousands of African Americans from voting.[9] Long lines and other kinds of disenfranchisement were experienced in at least two dozen states.[10] More than one third of the provisional ballots cast by people who showed up at the polls determined to vote were not counted.[11] Potentially most damning of all, a panel of highly respected academic statisticians examining contradictory exit poll data concluded that "all voting equipment technologies except paper ballots were associated with large unexplained exit poll discrepancies" in the 2004 Presidential election.[12] With a war-induced mainstream press blackout on questions of vote fraud, it was left to *Rolling Stone* magazine to ask: "Was the 2004 Election Stolen?"[13]

The right to vote is the most basic democratic right. Without it democracy is meaningless. But the right to vote is not a strict either-or dichotomy. Like all rights, it exists (and can be infringed) in varying degrees. Progressive public policy should always seek to encourage people to vote by ensuring that voting is as quick, easy, and unthreatening as possible. Polling stations should be welcoming, not hostile or forbidding. Election monitors should offer cookies, not challenges.

People have to vote where they live, not where they work, so elections should be held on weekends, not on workdays. Election Day is set by Federal law as a Tuesday, but this is not specified in the Constitution. It can be changed by Congress at any time. Voting hours should also be expanded, and more voters should be encouraged to vote early and vote by mail. Why not mail a registration form to everyone in America? Or even register people automatically and send them ballots? If junk mail companies can find us, so can state election agencies. Most importantly, no one should be turned away at the polls. If someone accidentally turns up at the wrong polling station, surely the information technology of the 21st century can handle the situation. States should be helping people vote, not preventing them from voting.

At least 24 states (including Florida and Ohio) have the technology to automatically issue traffic fines to people who run red lights.[14] They should have the technology to process votes from people whose drivers' licenses contain out of date information. After all, a maiden name on a drivers' license won't get you out of a traffic ticket. It shouldn't bar you from voting.

Voter suppression is antithetical to democracy. It dishonors the extraordinary sacrifices that past generations of Americans have made to create, safeguard, and spread the right to vote from a few small British colonies to the rest of the world. Suppressing the vote in order to win an election is both petty and criminal. Petty it may be, but voter suppression is so widespread in the United States that it criminally undermines the integrity of our democracy. Progressives are right to fight for voters' rights. And for once the moral high ground is also the political high ground: The more people are able vote, the more progressives are likely to win.

14
STOP TORTURING, STOP ASSASSINATING, AND CLOSE DOWN THE NSA

"We tortured some folks. We did some things that were contrary to our values ... we did some things that were wrong."[1] That may be the understatement of the century so far, but at least it's an improvement on "[I] laid the foundation for peace by making some awfully difficult decisions."[2] Score Obama 1, Bush 0 in the acknowledgment of the torture game show. It's a start. There is no hiding the fact that America in the 21st century embraced torture as a routine tool of foreign policy—or if not torture, at least "cruel, inhuman, or degrading treatment or punishment" as long as it was not "equivalent in intensity to the pain accompanying serious physical injury, such as organ failure, impairment of bodily function, or even death." [3]

Torture (or extremely enhanced nontorture) techniques approved for use by the Central Intelligence Agency (CIA) in the War on Terror included waterboarding, keeping prisoners cold, naked, and wet, and sleep deprivation of up to 180 hours.[4] For the record, 180 hours equals seven and a half days. The pain accompanied by 180 hours without sleep may or may not be equivalent in intensity to the pain accompanying organ failure or death, but it can't be pleasant. No one said that interrogation should be pleasant, but no one said it had to be nasty. In any case there is no evidence that nasty works. The expert consensus is that it does not.[5] Whatever else it may be, keeping prisoners cold, naked, and wet without sleep for days on end certainly is not civilized. It is beneath the dignity of a civilized country. It is beneath the dignity of the United States of America. But the government of the United States of America does many things that are beneath the dignity of the United States of America.

It has, however, banned torture. On January 22, 2009 President Obama issued Executive Order 13491 banning torture by US government personnel. This order does not, however, ban US government personnel from subcontracting torture to third parties overseas.[6] Press reports suggest that so-called "extraordinary renditions" of prisoners to third countries with dubious human rights records continue.[7] Nor is this order binding on future Presidents, nor even on President Obama himself. Its legal status is more akin to a memo from a boss to all employees. The boss can always change his mind.

The logical next step beyond torture—especially if torture doesn't really work anyway—is just to kill people who are suspected of committing, planning, or even thinking about attacking the United States (and anyone with the bad judgment or bad luck to be found near them). On October 23, 2012 *Washington Post* journalist Greg Miller disclosed the existence of a "disposition matrix" or kill list maintained by the White House to facilitate the worldwide organization of targeted killings by the US government.[8] Targeted killing is widely understood as President Obama's alternative to President Bush's torture and rendition programs.[9] As Greg Miller put it in his original exposé, "Targeted killing is now so routine that the Obama administration has spent much of the past year codifying and streamlining the processes that sustain it."

Research from The Bureau of Investigative Journalism (TBIJ) indicates that US drone strikes kill roughly 10-12 people per month in Pakistan, every month. Figures tallied by TBIJ include 199-410 deaths in 2012, 108-195 deaths in 2013, and 51-77 deaths between January and June 2014.[10] Drone strikes also occur regularly in Yemen and Somalia, and presumably elsewhere in the region as well. The truth is that no one outside the US government really knows the extent of US drone strikes. The statistics compiled by TBIJ and other watchdogs are drawn from press reports, not comprehensive databases.

If targeted killing by drone aircraft is occurring and admitted by the US government, what other forms of targeted killing are occurring— or might occur in the future? That's the nub of the problem. Most

Americans seem not to be alarmed by the killing of a dozen people a month in remote parts of the world, even if many of those people are actually innocent of terrorism or hostility toward the United States. Pew Research Center polls consistently report solid bipartisan majorities in favor of extrajudicial drone killings.[11] But there is no special legal basis for killings by missiles launched from drone aircraft, as opposed to killings by knife, bullet, poison, or laser beam. Killing is killing. When the President of the United States claims the right to kill any enemy of the United States anywhere outside the United States, the world should pay attention.

And the world does. American drone strikes are wildly unpopular in almost every country surveyed by the Pew Research Global Attitudes Project.[12] Among populations surveyed, only Israelis and Kenyans strongly support American drone strikes (more so than Americans themselves). Populations in 40 other countries strongly disapprove. The world's concern is not about the trustworthiness of President Obama. The world likes Obama, in general more than Americans do.[13] The world's concern is for the next President, and the next, and the next. Once it becomes broadly accepted and well established the President of the United States has a license to kill, it will be very difficult to take that license away.

That a President cannot be prosecuted under US law for killing people abroad now seems clear. The President's Article II authority to order military action as commander-in-chief of the armed forces is now broadly accepted and well established. Only Congress can effectively discipline the President, and it is unlikely that any Congress would ever impeach a President on behalf of foreigners (or even the occasional American) killed in foreign countries. That a President of the United States would ever be successfully prosecuted under international law is equally unlikely. But a confidently progressive President of the United States could renounce the authority to kill individuals abroad, as Presidents Ford and Carter did through executive orders in the 1970s. If a succession of Presidents reinforced this ban, it might be very difficult for a future President to claim a Constitutional privilege to resume targeted killings in the pursuit of national security.

The shift to a more restrained foreign policy based on the rule of law won't take place overnight, but it can start in 2016. Americans are tired of the never-ending War on Terror, with more than half agreeing that "the US should mind its own business internationally," the higher percentage ever recorded.[14] If there ever was a right time for a Presidential candidate to tear up the license to kill, it is now.

Targeted drone killings are the thunderous hammer blows of Presidential power. The all-pervasive surveillance state is the solid steel anvil on which they fall. The power to kill would hardly matter without the ability to locate. It is no coincidence that GPS killing by drone strikes arose in conjunction with the emergence of the electronic surveillance state. Many organs of the federal government are tied into the surveillance state, but the nervous system of the surveillance state is the National Security Agency (NSA). The NSA is the federal agency charged with exclusive control over the country's signals intelligence.[15]

Signals intelligence is "intelligence derived from electronic signals and systems used by foreign targets, such as communications systems, radars, and weapons systems" and the NSA's mission in this regard "is specifically limited to gathering information about international terrorists and foreign powers, organizations, or persons."[16] At least that's what the website says. Thanks to the revelations of Edward Snowden and other whistleblowers, we all now know that "systems used by foreign targets" include not just "communications systems, radars, and weapons systems" but also phone calls, emails, browsing records, and pretty much everything everyone does on the internet. The chances are that you are using a system used by foreign targets right now. And chances are the NSA is recording that fact.

In a globalized world it is little comfort that the NSA's mission "is specifically limited to gathering information about international terrorists" (perhaps a few thousand people) and "foreign powers, organizations, or persons" (most of the rest of the population of the planet). Do you have any social network ties with foreigners (e.g., Canadians or Mexicans)? Do you have any accounts with foreign organizations (e.g., your bank, brokerage, or credit card company)? Do you ever travel outside the United States? If so, you may legally be in the NSA's databases too. In fact, Snowden revealed that pretty much everyone is in the NSA's databases, a fact confirmed by President Obama himself.[17] The data may not always be accessed or acted upon. But it is there.

It shouldn't be. In the 21st century the NSA has grown from a sleepy Maryland codebreaking operation and host of the National Cryptologic Museum into an $11 billion a year behemoth.[18] To help house all its newfound data it has built a massive $2 billion data center in the Utah desert capable of storing information on every aspect of our lives.[19] Not that the data center actually works. Built and managed by private contractors under the expert supervision of the Army Corps of Engineers, the Utah data center has experienced repeated electrical surges that have delayed the project by more than a year and melted down computer equipment worth hundreds of thousands of taxpayers' dollars.[20]

Whether or not the data center ultimately comes online and whether or not the NSA purposely spies on Americans, since the beginning of the century it has dramatically shifted the focus of its operations. It still monitors the satellite communications of foreign armed forces (one hopes), but now it also seeks to monitor the email, web browsing, and phone records of the entire world. In the 21st century and beyond this may be feasible, but is it desirable? Should a government monitor the entire world's electronic communications just because it can? In the 18th century it was feasible for a government to monitor all its people's postal communications. Some governments chose not to. The 4th Amendment to the United States Constitution expressly forbad the US government from opening our physical paper mail without a court-issued search warrant. The idea that the government should have access to all our communications "just in case" it needed it to fight terrorism would have been anathema to American founding fathers like Samuel Adams, Patrick Henry, and Benjamin Franklin.

Since the turn of the century the NSA has run amok with our privacy. It must be reined in. Its traditional activities should be handed over to formal military control and its civilian activities should be put to an end. The NSA itself should be disbanded. It has lost its way, and in the process its credibility. It is time to start over. And without the NSA anvil to fall on, the CIA hammer would lose much of its force. The CIA is only able to target and kill people via drone strikes because it (thinks it) can identify them in the hazy cloud of global communications. Remove the (often false) certainty that comes from picking up a cell phone signal emanating from an unmarked car observed from 10,000 feet and the CIA would have to return to killing people the old-fashioned way: in person. Without the ease of drone warfare, the CIA would have to go back to killing far fewer people and by extension killing far fewer innocent people. The decision to kill would once again be an extreme manifestation of national security policy taken on an exceptional basis, not a routine take-away deliverable from a gruesome weekly PowerPoint presentation.[21]

What does it mean to be the leader of the free world when the free world has become a world of torture, targeted killing, and mass surveillance? Surely under such circumstances the word "free" is in desperate need of renewal. The United States risks its reputation (and much more) if it keeps using death as the default instrument of foreign policy. The oppression business is fundamentally un-American. It does us no demonstrable good and makes us hated and feared around the world. It probably fosters more terrorism than it prevents. And it just isn't us. Our country and our consciences would be better off if America had a more dignified system of national security. We might even be more secure.

15
SUFFER THE REFUGEE CHILDREN

Suffer the little children to come unto me, and forbid them not: for of such is the kingdom of God. (Mark 10:14)

That's suffer as in "let them impose on you," not suffer as in "make them suffer." As the nursery song says, "Jesus loves the little children."[1] Even, one must suppose, Unaccompanied Alien Children from Central America. Over the 11 months from October, 2013 to August, 2014 at least 66,127 "Unaccompanied Alien Children from Central America" (as the Department of Homeland Security calls them) arrived uninvited on America's southern border. The combined totals for fiscal years 2013 and 2014 run to over 100,000.[2] Another 80,000 people arrived as families, mainly women with children, and promptly turned themselves in. These are not people running from Customs and Border Protection. They are seeking border protection.

Mixed in with these statistics are a steady trickle of 10,000-20,000 children arriving every year from Mexico who mostly do try to evade Customs and Border Protection. These are mainly teenage boys under the age of 18 who are legally children, but in the public imagination seem more like young men. Children like these have been crossing the border for decades seeking work in the United States. The current crisis includes them but isn't mainly about them. The current crisis is mainly about the flood of Central American children, nearly all of them from El Salvador, Guatemala, and Honduras but also some from southern Mexico and elsewhere in Central America, who are unambiguously being sent north by their families in hopes of saving their lives.

These are not migrants. These are refugees. Most Americans understand this. The results of a recent survey suggest that 69% of

Americans "say that children arriving from Central America should be treated as refugees and allowed to stay in the US if authorities determine it is not safe for them to return to their home countries."[3] The same survey from the Public Religion Research Institute shows that 71% of Americans "agree that while children from Central America are waiting for their cases to be heard, they should be released to the care of relatives, host families or churches, rather than be detained by immigration authorities."

A refugee is any person who "owing to well-founded fear of being persecuted for reasons of race, religion, nationality, membership of a particular social group or political opinion, is outside the country of his nationality and is unable or, owing to such fear, is unwilling to avail himself of the protection of that country."[4] In international law a person who migrates to find a better life is not a refugee. Nor is someone who flees personal troubles, for example someone who is afraid of street crime, no matter how severe the threat. Such people may have very good reasons for migrating, and may deserve our sympathy and assistance, but technically speaking they are not refugees.

Most of the current wave of refugees from Central America are not economic migrants or even migrants from crime but are fleeing persecution on the basis of "membership of a particular social group." That group is the indigenous: the Native Americans, American Indians, First Peoples, Mayans, or whatever you want to call the original inhabitants of Central America. The current wave of Central American refugees are almost all indigenous people in countries where indigenous peoples have long faced severe persecution bordering on genocide. When news reports say that child refugees come from "poor, rural areas" that is really Central American code language for indigenous people. Virtually all of the poor, rural people of Central America are indigenous, and most of the urban slum-dwellers are just poor, rural people who have previously been forced off their land.

What the United States of America did to its indigenous people more than 100 years ago, the governments, militias, death squads, and drug gangs of Central America are doing to their indigenous peoples right now. In some parts of Central America governments, paramilitary militias, death squads, and drug gangs may actually be one and the same. For the indigenous peoples of Central America, just as for the Native American nations of the 19th century, there really is no one to turn to and nowhere to hide. The powerful miners, cattle ranchers, and drug traffickers who lord over them would prefer if they just disappeared—or actively work to disappear them.

In many ways the repressive forces of Central America are just like the Islamic State terrorists of Iraq and Syria, except that they do not usually claim to act in the name of religion. Just like the Islamic State they use rape, torture, mutilation, beheadings, and mass murder to intimidate local populations into submission.[5] Indigenous villagers and slum-dwellers are given the same stark choice that the Islamic State gives to Syrians and Iraqis: join us or die.[6] Young girls in particular face the most extremely brutal forms of violence, involving not "just" rape but highly sexualized killings[7] involving mutilation and dismemberment.

Indigenous people have faced severe persecution in Central America ever since the Spanish conquistadors arrived more than five centuries ago, but persecution based on indigeneity has gone largely unnoted in media accounts of the child refugee crisis. Even the United Nations High Commissioner for Refugees[8] and the United States Conference of Catholic Bishops[9] make only passing mention of it in their reports on the crisis. The statistics in their reports identify as indigenous only children who actually speak Mayan languages. It is true that many of the indigenous peoples of Central America are the decedents of the ancient Mayan civilization and many of them still speak Mayan languages. But just as most Native American children in the United States now only speak English, most indigenous people in Central America now only speak Spanish. That doesn't make them any less indigenous. It certainly doesn't make them any less persecuted.

The targeted persecution of indigenous peoples in Central America may make most of the "Unaccompanied Alien Children from Central America" refugees in the terminology of international law, but it does not make them refugees under US law. Under US law, you can't be a refugee if you are already in the United States. By definition, in the United States a refugee can only be someone who is "located outside of the United States" and is "of special humanitarian concern to the United States."[10] Sorry, Unaccompanied Alien Children from Central America: If you are a bona fide refugee but you are already inside the United States the best you can hope for is to become an asylum seeker. Just file form I-589, Application for Asylum and Withholding of Removal. Good luck. Reports suggest that asylum application success rates for people from El Salvador, Guatemala, and Honduras hover somewhere between 4% and 7%.[11] Success rates for refugees from Mexico are even lower.

Contrast that with the assistance given to refugees from the Syrian civil war. Turkey has accepted more than one million refugees from Syria, including refugees from Islamic State attacks. Lebanon has accepted more than a million refugees and Jordan more than half a million.[12] These millions of Syrian refugees have been greeted, if not exactly with open arms, then at least with food, schools, and sympathy. Virtually none of them applied for admission before arriving at the border. They just showed up. The United States—with more than three times the population and ten times the wealth of Turkey, Lebanon, and Jordan combined—has been confronted with some 100,000 to 200,000 child refugees from civil unrest in Mexico and Central America. None of them has an automatic right to protection on US soil. All of them face an uncertain future including potential deportation. Many of them have been greeted with protests and jeers on their way to immigration detention centers.[13]

What's wrong with this picture?

The United States likes to think of itself as a country that does good in the world and the American people like to think of themselves as humane and charitable in their daily lives. But with charity as with smartphones and flat-screen televisions Americans tend to demand consumer choice. We're willing to give, and give a lot, as long as we get to decide who to give to and when. Refugees like those arriving from Central America take that choice away. They don't let us decide whether or not to give. Who can turn down a child on the doorstep? There have been press reports of people who do, but these are a tiny minority of Americans. According to the Public Religion Research Institute poll cited above, even a majority of Republicans (52%) believe that the Central American children should be treated as refugees. Independents (69%) and Democrats (80%) gave even higher levels of support.[14]

Though some Americans may be angry at being forced to offer charity, most people understand that parents don't send their children alone or in the hands of people smugglers on dangerous journeys across national borders unless they have serious worries about their children's lives. If charity begins at home, the "Unaccompanied Alien Children from Central America" are here, in our homes, literally crying for charity. The progressive thing to do is the only human thing to do: to care for them as we would our own children. A progressive president who exhorts Americans to open their hearts to refugee children fleeing violence in Central America will tap into an enormous reservoir of goodwill—and save taxpayer money while doing so. The vast majority of these children have been sent by their parents to join family members already in the United States.[15] These relatives will gladly take on the burden of caring for them if they are allowed to do so. Why process children and their families for deportation when people already living in America desperately want to have the opportunity to provide for them?

Goodness may not make headlines, but goodness is popular. If ever there was a campaign issue that clearly distinguishes good from evil, it is the treatment of refugee children. A progressive candidate could and should use this issue to firmly establish progressivism as the family values platform it really is.

Just as Syria's neighbors cannot save every oppressed family in Syria, the United States cannot save every oppressed family in Central America. There are just too many. But we can do more than we are doing. And recognizing our responsibility to care for the children on our doorsteps would be a good first step toward recognizing our responsibility to address the problems that have created the crisis: oppressive political factions, rampant illegal gun exports, and, most of all, the drug wars. Too many of these problems are "Made in America."

The vilification of refugee children is a cheap way to win cheap votes, and in fact President Obama has found it very difficult to address the child refugee crisis because of cheap hits from political rivals. As usual, Congress is in no mood to help. But deep down Americans really are charitable, Americans really are generous, and Americans really are eager to do good in the world and have good done on their behalf. If and when voters are offered a straight-up electoral choice between a generous progressive and a mean conservative, there is every reason to think that they will chose the progressive. A progressive Presidential candidate should recognize this, and help lead us toward our better selves. Helping children is a potential vote winner, not just another thankless duty of responsible leadership. But either way it is a duty of leadership and progressives should take the lead in 2016, on this issue of all issues. Progressives should stake their claim on the moral high ground and let the world know that America is proud to care.

> **Ye are the light of the world. A city that is set on an hill cannot be hid. Neither do men light a candle, and put it under a bushel, but on a candlestick; and it giveth light unto all that are in the house. Let your light so shine before men, that they may see your good works. (Matthew 5:14-16)**

16
SAVE THE EARTH

The Earth is dying. That is not hyperbole. That is reality.

Human beings are torturing the Earth to extract every ounce of useful mineral. We are scouring the land to produce just one more crop before the soil gives out. We are fishing the oceans clean of every living thing that is tastier than a jellyfish. We are depleting every aquifer, felling every tree, feeding every last blade of grass to a cow to be slaughtered for meat, leather, and assorted industrial products. Whatever is left we are killing with global warming, and remember that we are still in the early stages of global warming. The world has only been warming since around 1980.[1] It is now warming very rapidly indeed. Under any likely scenario, there is no end in sight.[2]

Global warming is caused by the burning of fossil fuels.[3] It's very simple really. Digging things up and burning them takes carbon out of the ground and puts it into the atmosphere. Carbon dioxide and other gasses in the atmosphere trap warmth through a well-understood and universally accepted mechanism called the greenhouse effect.[4] It is as if the Earth were covered by a planetary carbon quilt. It is theoretically conceivable that the most of the new carbon entering the Earth's atmosphere is coming from natural sources or that human beings have not yet added enough carbon to the atmosphere to cause a greenhouse effect. But it is not theoretically conceivable that human beings could add infinite amounts of carbon to the atmosphere without causing a greenhouse effect.

Given that carbon dioxide levels are known to cause a greenhouse effect, that carbon dioxide levels are known to be rising, and that burning fossil fuels is known to release carbon dioxide, it seems pretty reasonable to connect the dots and conclude that rising global temperatures are related to the burning of fossil fuels. Even if the real truth (suppressed by climate scientists the world over) is that global warming to date has not been caused by the burning of fossil fuels, this does not imply that it is safe to burn all of the remaining fossil fuels that are still buried in the Earth's crust. At some point global warming must kick in. Most people agree that we are already well past that point: 67% of Americans agree that there is "solid evidence" that the Earth is warming.[5]

Nonetheless, human beings really are on course to extract all fossil fuels, wherever they are, anywhere in the world. No deposit of oil, coal, or natural gas is too deep, too remote, or too diffuse to keep us from getting it out of the ground and burning it. Anything existing in or on the surface of the Earth that can be burned, will be burned. If we find similar hydrocarbons on other planets we will burn them, too.[6]

Case in point: the Canadian tar sands. Tar sands are "a combination of clay, sand, water, and bitumen, a heavy black viscous oil."[7] They are mined in giant open-pit mines or by pumping hot water into the ground to scald the oil out of the solid rock. Roughly two tons of sand must be mined to extract one barrel of oil. The Canadian tar sands hold proven reserved 168 billion barrels of oil.[8] Don't bother doing the math. Tar sands companies in Alberta are required to "conserve and reclaim disturbed land to an equivalent land capability" as before mining.[9] The Athabasca tar sands mine has been in operation since 1967; despite the fact that grass has been planted over completed mining sites, NASA satellite imagery has shown no plant growth to date.[10] This may or may not be related to the fact that it just so happens that in Alberta formal criteria "that may be used to evaluate reclamation success are not yet defined."[11]

The Athabasca tar sands are at heart of the controversial Keystone XL pipeline project to transport oil from Canada to the US Gulf coast that former NASA scientist James Hansen has famously called "game over" for the Earth's climate.[12] Tar sands may be about as bad as things gets for the environment, but conventional sources of fossil fuels aren't that much better. Who could forget the 2010 Deepwater Horizon spill in the Gulf of Mexico? The Environmental Protection Agency estimates that 4.9 million barrels of oil were released into the ocean as a result of this single accident.[13]

The Deepwater Horizon drilling rig was not one of a kind. There are at least 700 drilling vessels actively contracted to drill for oil somewhere in the world at any one time, about 10% of them operating in the Gulf of Mexico.[14] And these vessels just drill the wells. No one knows how many offshore platforms are out there pumping oil to the surface. Suffice it to say that if there are more than 700 vessels actively drilling new wells, there are thousands of platforms pumping up the oil they find. Offshore oil drilling in the Gulf of Mexico can involve platforms anchored to the seabed as much as 9,000 feet below.[15] For comparison, the Empire State Building is 1,454 feet tall, spire and all. Pipes run from these platforms nearly two miles down to the seabed and then another mile or two (or three) under the seabed to the oil itself. In the most extreme example, in Brazil's Carcará oil field, oil is brought up through 27,000 feet (more than five miles) of piping to a surface platform before being loaded onto tankers to be brought to land.[16]

As if this weren't extreme enough, along came fracking. Hydraulic fracturing—"fracking"—involves the pumping of millions of gallons of chemical-laced water into the ground in order to crack open rocks so that tiny bubbles of natural gas trapped inside them can be liberated and brought up to the surface. Does this sound like a good idea? Thousands of fracking-induced earthquakes say no.[17]

Sensible or not, fracking is only economical for two reasons. First, in the 1990s the development of directional drilling made it possible to drill a gas well that follows the contours of the narrow shale formations in which shale gas is trapped.[18] Second, in 2005 Congress specifically exempted "hydraulic fracturing operations" from regulation by the Environmental Protection Agency.[19] Various aspects of fracking operations are exempted from the Clean Air Act, the Clean Water Act, the Safe Drinking Water Act, the Resource Conservation and Recovery Act, the Comprehensive Environmental Response, Compensation, and Liability ("Superfund") Act, the National Environmental Policy Act, and the Emergency Planning and Community Right-to-Know Act.[20] That's right: frackers can poison your water and you have no right to know about it, never mind do anything about it.

Josh Fox's 2010 documentary *Gasland* made flammable drinking water and exploding kitchen taps a staple of internet video entertainment. But 2010 was just the beginning of the fracking boom. Natural gas extraction from the Marcellus shale formation (on which Fox's land sits) expanded by more than 650% between 2010 and 2014—and is still growing rapidly.[21] Shale gas reserves in the state of New York haven't even been tapped yet, but could be at any time. ProPublica suggests that a revision of the New York fracking moratorium could be forthcoming as soon as 2015.[22] Given that shale gas is estimated to form nearly one third of the world's recoverable natural gas reserves, it is almost certain that fracking is here to stay.[23]

And then there's coal. It is hard to believe that such a thing as mountaintop removal mining actually exists, but there it is. Even the most serious official sources cannot resist a wry chuckle at its very name: "As its name suggests, mountaintop removal mining involves removing the top of a mountain in order to recover the coal seams contained in the mountain."[24] The one ton of coal extracted per 16 tons of mountain displaced makes mountaintop removal roughly as efficient tar sands, give or take a ton of spoilage.[25]

Though recent data are hard to come by, mountaintop removal mines approved between 1992 and 2002 were projected to destroy at least 1,200 miles of streams, and the Environmental Protection Agency estimates that mines approved between 2002 and 2012 will have roughly the same impact.[26] Mountaintop removal started before 1992 and continued after 2012, so well over 2,400 miles of streams have been written off so far. They won't be coming back. Neither will the mountains. That's the thing about mountains: No one is building new ones, at least not in our lifetimes. Entire mountains the size of small cities are being destroyed forever in return for a maximum of 10-15 years of mining productivity.[27] That is nothing short of madness—unless, of course, you like to hunt elk or play golf on the newly flattened land.[28] At least three golf courses have been built on former mountaintop removal sites across Appalachia.[29]

Tar sands, offshore oil, shale gas, and coal mining: All this means carbon, and carbon of the worst kind. Getting oil from tar sands produces more greenhouse gas emissions than just about any other kind of oil.[30] Offshore oil drilling is set for major expansion as—irony of ironies—global warming melts the Arctic icecap.[31] Natural gas derived from fracking may promote global warming even more than coal due to gas seepage during the extraction process—unburned natural gas has 25 times the greenhouse effect of carbon dioxide.[32] And of course, coal is coal. Forget about 2 degrees Celsius and forget about mere "climate change";the way things are going the Earth will eventually become a Venus-like hell planet in which Americans and other rich people live in protected bubble cities while the rest of the world descends into famine and chaos. Some might say that this process has already started.

Don't look to geoengineering to provide a solution. Geoengineering is the idea that we should reverse global warming by dumping yet more pollutants into the environment. The goal of geoengineering is to offset the warming caused by carbon dioxide and other greenhouse gasses with an equal amount of cooling caused by alternative forms of human intervention to produce a perfectly balanced climate, kept in perpetual equilibrium through effective expert management. That's right: Conservatives don't trust the government to run a healthcare website, but they trust the government to run the climate—and not just our climate: the whole world's climate. Not that we've asked the rest of the world how they feel about this. Or will we turn the Earth's climate over to the United Nations to manage? The idea that we will provoke artificial volcanic eruptions or install millions of tiny mirrors in space just so we can keep driving our trucks and SUVs is simply pathological.

If Hollywood is right, whenever aliens invade the Earth, America comes to the rescue. America made the world safe for democracy in World War I, defeated Fascism in World War II, and undermined Communism while avoiding World War III. President Bush launched a global War on Terror that President Obama is still fighting today. Maybe it is time for a different kind of war, or better yet, a plan. We need a plan to stop global warming, if not now then soon. We need to get our of our cars, and to do that we need to relearn how to live together in ways that don't require cars. We need to keep the Earth's remaining fossil fuels firmly in the ground. We need to burn less and plant more.

It is almost certainly too late to prevent catastrophic global warming. It is perhaps not too late to save the Earth itself. There is no cause more progressive than environmental stewardship. There should be no cause more conservative than conservation. If government of the people, by the people, for the people is not to perish from the Earth then there must be an Earth. It is our responsibility to work together to ensure that there is.

Notes

Chapter 1

[1] Calculations based on Bureau of Labor Statistics Employment Situation Summary Table A-8.

[2] Calculations based on Bureau of Labor Statistics Employment Situation Summary Table A-1.

[3] Calculations based on Bureau of Labor Statistics Employment Situation Summary Table A-1.

[4] National Bureau of Economic Research, US Business Cycle Expansions and Contractions, September 20, 2010.

[5] Bureau of Economic Analysis, National Income and Product Accounts, Table 1.1.1.

[6] Bureau of Economic Analysis, National Income and Product Accounts, Table 1.1.1.

[7] Benjamin Snyder, Dow Closes at Another Record High on a Day Dominated by Alibaba, *Fortune*, September 19, 2014.

[8] Connie R. Wanberg, The Individual Experience of Unemployment, *Annual Review of Psychology*, 2012, 63:369-96.

[9] David J. Roelfs, Eran Shor, Karina W. Davidson, and Joseph E. Schwartz, Losing Life and Livelihood: A Systematic Review and Meta-Analysis of Unemployment and All-Cause Mortality, *Social Science & Medicine*, 2011, 72:840-54.

[10] Jeanne Brooks-Gunn, William Schneider, and Jane Waldfogel, The Great Recession and the Risk for Child Maltreatment, *Child Abuse & Neglect*, 2013, 37:721-9.

[11] National Bureau of Economic Research, US Business Cycle Expansions and Contractions, September 20, 2010.

[12] Calculations based on Bureau of Labor Statistics Employment Situation Summary Table A-1.

[13] Bureau of Economic Analysis, National Income and Product Accounts, Table 1.12.

[14] Daniel J. Wilson, Fiscal Spending Jobs Multipliers: Evidence from the 2009 American Recovery and Reinvestment Act, *American Economic Journal: Economic Policy*, 2012, 4:251-82.

[15] Rick Ungar, The Truth About the Bush Tax Cuts and Job Growth, *Forbes*, July 17, 2012.

[16] Congressional Budget Office, Comparing the Compensation of Federal and Private-Sector Employees, January 2012.

[17] Calculations based on Office of Management and the Budget Table 1.1. Summary of Receipts, Outlays, and Surpluses or Deficits: 1789–2019.

[18] Mark Zandi, A Second Quick Boost From Government Could Spark Recovery, *Moody's Analytics*, July 24, 2008.

[19] Robert Pollin and Heidi Garrett-Peltier, *The US Employment Effects of Military and Domestic Spending Priorities: 2011 Update*, Political Economy Research Institute, University of Massachusetts, December, 2011, p. 6.

[20] Michael R. Darby, Three-and-a-Half Million US Employees Have Been Mislaid: Or, an Explanation of Unemployment, 1934-1941, *Journal of Political Economy*,1976, 84: 7.

Chapter 2

[1] Calculations based on Bureau of Labor Statistics Employment Situation Summary Table A-1.

[2] Census Bureau Historical Income Tables Table P-8.

[3] Calculations based on Census Bureau Historical Poverty Tables Table 2.

[4] Bureau of Labor Statistics CPI-U historical data.

[5] Calculations based on Bureau of Labor Statistics Employment Situation Summary Table B-1

[6] Laura Choi, *For-Profit Colleges and the Student Debt Crisis*, Federal Reserve Bank of San Francisco, January 10, 2014.

[7] Stephen Barrett, Dubious Medical Tests, Quackwatch, retrieved September 30, 2014.

[8] Andrew L. Spivak and Susan F. Sharp, Inmate Recidivism as a Measure of Private Prison Performance, *Crime & Delinquency*, 2008, 54:482-508.

[9] Child Trends Data Bank 2012; calculations based on Census Bureau data.

[10] Department of Health and Human Services Head Start Program Facts Fiscal Year 2012.

[11] Calculations based on Bureau of Labor Statistics Employment Situation Summary Table B-1.

[12] Calculations based on Bureau of Labor Statistics Employment Situation Summary Table B-1.

[13] Calculations based on National Center for Education Statistics Elementary/Secondary Information System Express Tables for the 2010-11 school year.

[14] National Center for Health Statistics, Health, United States, Table 105.

[15] Calculations based on data from the Census Bureau International Data Base.

[16] National Center for Health Statistics Health, United States, Table 105.

[17] Centers for Disease Control and Prevention, Oral and Dental Health, May 14, 2014.

[18] National Park Service, National Register of Historic Places Listed Properties (Up to June 2014), author's count.

Chapter 3

[1] Rachel Aviv, Wrong Answer, *New Yorker*, July 21, 2014.

[2] David P. Gardner et al, *A Nation at Risk*, National Commission on Excellence in Education, April 26, 1983.

[3] Gary Miron and Charisse Gulosino, Profiles of For-Profit and Not-For-Profit Education Management Organizations, National Education Policy Center, November 2013, p i.

[4] Stephanie Strom, For School Company, Issues of Money and Control, *New York Times*, April 23, 2010.

[5] Paul Buchheit, The 4 Most Profound Ways Privatization Perverts Education, *Alternet*, February 16, 2014.

[6] National Center for Education Statistics, The Evaluation of Charter School Impacts: Final Report, 2011.

[7] National Assessment of Educational Progress, The Nation's Report Card, Long Term Trend, Summary of Major Findings, accessed September 30, 2014.

[8] National Center for Education Statistics, US States in a Global Context: Results from the 2011 NAEP-TIMSS Linking Study, 2011.

Chapter 4

[1] Gerald Friedman, Funding HR 676: The Expanded and Improved Medicare for All Act: How We Can Afford a National Single-Payer Health Plan, Physicians for a National Health Program, July 31, 2013.

[2] Centers for Medicare & Medicaid Services National Health Expenditure Data Table 6.

[3] Patricia A. Davis et al, *Medicare Primer*, Congressional Research Service report R40425, January 31, 2013.

[4] National Committee to Preserve Social Security & Medicare, Issue Brief - Medicare Drug Negotiation and Rebates, retrieved September 30, 2014.

[5] Dean Baker, Reducing Waste with an Efficient Medicare Prescription Drug Benefit, Center for Economic and Policy Research, January 2013.

[6] Kimberly J. Morgan, Doomed from the Start, *Foreign Affairs*, October 17, 2013.

[7] John Holahan et al, The Launch of the Affordable Care Act in Selected States: State Flexibility is Leading to Very Different Outcomes, Urban Institute, March 2014.

[8] Peter A. Corning, The Evolution of Medicare ... from Idea to Law, Social Security History online archives, 1969, Chapter 4.

[10] Sara Rosenbaum, Lara Cartwright-Smith, Joel Hirsh, and Philip S. Mehler, Case Studies At Denver Health: "Patient Dumping" in the Emergency Department Despite EMTALA, the Law that Banned It, *Health Affairs*, 2012, 31:1749.

[11] Phil Galewitz, Hospitals Demand Payment Upfront From ER Patients With Routine Problems, *Kaiser Health News*, February 20, 2012.

[12] Centers for Medicare & Medicaid Services, CMS FastFacts, July 2014.

[13] Kaiser Family Foundation, Status of State Action on the Medicaid Expansion Decision, 2014.

[14] Kaiser Family Foundation, Medicaid-to-Medicare Fee Index, 2012.

[15] Sandra L. Decker, In 2011 Nearly One-Third of Physicians Said They Would Not Accept New Medicaid Patients, but Rising Fees May Help, *Health Affairs*, 2012, 31:1673-1679.

[16] Taubman et al, Medicaid Increases Emergency-Department Use: Evidence from Oregon's Health Insurance Experiment, *Science*, 2014, 343:263-268.

[17] Centers for Medicare & Medicaid Services National Health Expenditure Data Table 22.

[18] Census Bureau, Current Population Survey Annual Social and Economic Supplement Table HI01. Health Insurance Coverage Status and Type of Coverage by Selected Characteristics: 2012.

[19] Kaiser Family Foundation, Medicare Advantage Fact Sheet, 2013.

[20] The Advisory Board Company, Pay for Health Care CEOs Exceeds All Other Industries, 2013.

[21] Biles et al, The Continuing Cost of Privatization: Extra Payments to Medicare Advantage Plans Jump to $11.4 Billion in 2009, The Commonwealth Fund, 2009.

[22] Kip Sullivan, Two-Thirds of Americans Support Medicare for All, Physicians for a National Health Program, 2009, page 5.

[23] Aaron E. Carroll and Ronald T. Ackerman, Support for National Health Insurance among US Physicians: 5 Years Later, *Annals of Internal Medicine*, 2008, 148:566-7.

Chapter 5

[1] Calculations based on IRS, SOI Tax Stats—Individual Statistical Tables by Size of Adjusted Gross Income, Individual Complete Report (Publication 1304), Table 1.1, 1996.

[2] Calculations based on IRS, SOI Tax Stats—Individual Statistical Tables by Size of Adjusted Gross Income, Individual Complete Report (Publication 1304), Table 1.1, 2012.

[3] Rebecca Thiess, The Bush Tax Cuts Are Here to Stay, Economic Policy Institute, January 7, 2013.

[4] Zachary R. Mider, How Wal-Mart's Waltons Maintain Their Billionaire Fortune, Bloomberg, September 12, 2013.

[5] Alexander Arapoglou and Jerri-Lynn Scofield, 10 Tax Dodges that Help the Rich Get Richer, *Salon*, April 13, 2013.

[6] Calculations based on World Top Incomes Database, variable 6310501.

[7] Calculations based on World Top Incomes Database, variable 1210501.

[8] Office of Management and Budget, Historical Table 2.3: Receipts by Source as Percentages of GDP: 1934-2019.

[9] Office of Management and Budget, Historical Table 2.3: Receipts by Source as Percentages of GDP: 1934-2019.

[10] IRS, SOI Tax Stats—Historical Table 23. US Individual Income Tax: Personal Exemptions and Lowest and Highest Bracket Tax Rates, and Tax Base for Regular Tax, Tax Years 1913-2012.

[11] Calculations based on a turnover between generations every 30 years and a very conservative 3% real return on investment; a 5% real return on investment allows the family to withdraw more than $37 million a year.

Chapter 6

[1] Social Security Administration, A Summary of the 2014 Annual Reports, Social Security and Medicare Boards of Trustees, retrieved September 30, 2014.

[2] David C. John, Misleading the Public: How the Social Security Trust Fund Really Works, The Heritage Foundation, September 2, 2004.

[3] Calculations based on IRS SOI Tax Stats - Individual Statistical Tables by Size of Adjusted Gross Income, Individual Complete Report (Publication 1304), Table 1.1, 2011.

NOTES

[4] Tax Policy Center, Tax Units with Zero or Negative Tax Liability, *Current Law*, 2004-2011, 2011.

[5] Brad Plumer, Who Doesn't Pay Taxes, in Eight Charts, *Washington Post*, September 18, 2012.

[6] Calculations based on Employment Situation Summary Table A. Household Data, 2013.

[7] Thomas L. Hungerford and Rebecca Thiess, The Earned Income Tax Credit and the Child Tax Credit, Economic Policy Institute issue brief 370, September 25, 2013.

[8] The 2010 Affordable Care Act created additional taxes that are also called Medicare taxes, but they are not part of the FICA wage tax system discussed here.

[9] A small number of state and municipal employees are exempt from FICA for technical historical reasons.

[10] Congressional Budget Office, The Distribution of Household Income and Federal Taxes, 2010, Table 2, 2013.

[11] Zach Carter, Mitt Romney Tax Returns for 2011 Released (update), The Huffington Post, September 21, 2012.

[12] Office of Management and Budget, Historical Table 2.1: Receipts by Source, 1934-2019 and Historical Table 2.2: Percentage Composition of Receipts by Source, 1934-2019.

[13] Office of Management and Budget, Historical Table 3.1: Outlays by Superfunction and Function, 1940-2019.

[14] Under the administration's proposal, all manual workers would be covered no matter what their wages but white-collar workers would be covered only if they made less than $250 per month ($3,000 per year), the implication being that low-wage secretaries and typists would be covered but not high-wage managers and executives; see Francis Perkins et al, Report of the Committee on Economic Security, Social Security Administration archives, 1935.

[15] Estimate based on figures from Janemarie Mulvey, *Social Security: Raising or Eliminating the Taxable Earnings Base*, Congressional Research Service report RL32896, 2010.

Chapter 7

[1] Office of the New York State Comptroller Thomas P. DiNapoli, Wall Street Bonuses Went Up In 2013 (press release), March 12, 2014.

[2] Office of the New York State Comptroller Thomas P. DiNapoli, Average Salaries In New York City Securities Industry vs. All Other Private Sector Industries, 2013.

[3] Roben Farzad, Goldman Sachs: Don't Blame Us, *Bloomberg Businessweek*, April 1, 2010.

[4] Citigroup CEO Vikram Pandit, quoted by Henry "Hank" Paulson, *On the Brink: Inside the Race to Stop the Collapse of the Global Financial System*, Hachette Book Group, 2010, page 365.

[5] Pew Research Center for the People & the Press, The People and Their Government: Distrust, Discontent, Anger, and Partisan Rancor, Section 1: Trust in Government 1958-2010, April 18, 2010.

[6] Calculations based on Bureau of Labor Statistics, Employment Situation Summary, Table A-1. Employment Status of the Civilian Population by Sex and Age, February 2014.

139

[7] Bureau of Labor Statistics, Employment Situation Summary Table A. Household Data, Seasonally Adjusted, February 2014.

[8] Geoffrey Rogow, Colocation: The Root of All High-Frequency Trading Evil? *Wall Street Journal* MarketBeat, September 20, 2012.

[9] Bob Ivry, Bradley Keoun, and Phil Kuntz, Secret Fed Loans Gave Banks $13 Billion Undisclosed to Congress, *Bloomberg*, November 28, 2011.

[10] Bloomberg News, The Fed's Secret Liquidity Lifelines, August 22, 2011.

[11] Paul Kiel and Dan Nguyen, The State of the Bailout, ProPublica, September 19, 2014.

[12] David Weidner, TARP: The Bailout Success Story that Wasn't, MarketWatch, February 12, 2013.

[13] Mark P. Keightley, *A Securities Transaction Tax: Financial Markets and Revenue Effects*, Congressional Research Service report R41192, Table 1, 2012.

Chapter 8

[1] Neal E. Boudette, Rivals Gear Up Ahead of Volkswagen Vote, *Wall Street Journal*, February 4, 2014.

[2] US Senate Committee on Health, Education, Labor, and Pensions, Alexander Statement on UAW Appeal of Chattanooga VW Vote (press release), February 21, 2014.

[3] Bureau of Labor Statistics, Local Area Employment Statistics, Employment Status of the Civilian Noninstitutional Population, Annual Averages, 2013.

[4] National Labor Relations Board, Right to Fair Representation, retrieved September 30, 2014.

[5] National Right to Work Legal Defense Foundation, Right to Work States, retrieved September 30, 2014.

[6] Barb Berggoetz, Right-to-Work Law: Now in the Hands of Indiana Supreme Court, *Indianapolis Star*, September 4, 2014.

[7] National Right to Work Legal Defense Foundation, Right to Work States, retrieved September 30, 2014.

[8] Barry Hirsch and David Macpherson, unionstats.com, Union Membership, Coverage, Density and Employment by State, 2013.

[9] Bill Koenig, UAW Ends NLRB Appeal of Volkswagen Union Vote, *Forbes*, April 21, 2014.

[10] National Right to Work Legal Defense Foundation press release, Volkswagen Workers' Brief Blasts UAW Bosses' Desperate and Delusional Attempt to Silence Dissenting Employees, April 3, 2014.

[11] David Bacon, The New Face of Unionbusting, Institute for Global Communications, retrieved September 20, 2014.

[12] David Madland and Karla Walter, The Employee Free Choice Act 101, Center for American Progress Action Fund, March 11, 2009.

[13] Chris Prandoni, AFL-CIO Throwing in Towel on Card Check, Americans for Tax Reform, April 29, 2010.

[14] Don McIntosh, Five Years in, Still no Flood of Unionization through Card Check, *Northwest Labor Press*, March 12, 2013.

Chapter 9

[1] Barack Obama, President Barack Obama's State of the Union Address, The White House, January 28, 2014.

[2] Lawrence Mishel, *Declining Value of the Federal Minimum Wage Is a Major Factor Driving Inequality*, Economic Policy Institute issue brief 351, February 21, 2013.

NOTES

3 Department of Health and Human Services, 2014 Poverty Guidelines, 2014 Poverty Guidelines for the 48 Contiguous States and the District of Columbia.

4 Board of Governors of the Federal Reserve System, Monetary Policy Press Release, January 25, 2012.

5 The President's speechwriters seem not to have thought to factor in a minor adjustment due to the fact that the calendar year actually consists of 52 weeks plus one day (two in leap years), not exactly 52 weeks.

6 Amy K. Glasmeier, West Arete, and Eric Schultheis, Living Wage Calculator, MIT Living Wage Project, March 24, 2014.

7 Gordon M. Fisher, The Development of the Orshansky Thresholds and Their Subsequent History as the Official US Poverty Measure, United States Census Bureau, 1992.

8 Calculation based on Bureau of the Census, Age and Sex Composition in the United States: 2012, Table 1.

9 Census Bureau, Historical Poverty Tables—People, Table 2: Poverty Status of People by Family Relationship, Race, and Hispanic Origin, 1959 to 2012.

10 Calculation based on Bureau of Economic Analysis, National Income and Product Accounts, Table 7.1.

11 Department of Labor, Wage and Hour Division, History of Federal Minimum Wage Rates Under the Fair Labor Standards Act, 1938-2009.

12 Calculation based on Bureau of Economic Analysis, National Income and Product Accounts, Table 7.1.

13 Dana Milbank, Raising the Minimum Wage without Raising Havoc, *Washington Post*, September 5, 2014.

14 Office of the Mayor, $15 Minimum Wage, City of Seattle, retrieved September 30, 2014.

15 Joel Connelly, Powerful D.C. Lobbies Join Fight against Seattle Minimum Wage, *Seattlepi*, August 13, 2014.

16 Department of Labor, Wage and Hour Division, Minimum Wage Laws in the States—January 1, 2014.

17 City of New York, Mayor de Blasio Signs Executive Order to Increase Living Wage and Expand it to Thousands More Workers, September 30, 2014.

18 Matt Flegenheimer, De Blasio's Executive Order Will Expand Living Wage Law to Thousands More, *New York Times*, September 29., 2014.

19 Franklin D. Roosevelt, State of the Union Address, Franklin D. Roosevelt Presidential Library and Museum, January 6, 1941.

Chapter 10

1 *National Lampoon* reportedly suggested "Putting the 'Execute' in Executive Branch" as a slogan for Governor Perry, but he is not known to have officially adopted it; Chuck Lewis, *National Lampoon*: Rick Perry Campaign Slogans, *Houston Chronicle*, August 22, 2011.

2 Henry J. Gomez, Rich Lowrie, Financial Planner behind Herman Cain's '9-9-9' Tax Plan: Whatever Happened to ...?, Northeast Ohio Media Group, March 10, 2013.

3 Amanda Terkel, Herman Cain 999 Plan: Did It Come From SimCity? Huffington Post, October 13, 2011.

4 Center for Public Integrity, PAC profile: 9-9-9 Fund, May 19, 2014.

5 David Freedlander, Is Herman Cain Running in 2016? The Daily Beast, May 31, 2014.

6 Aaron Sharockman, The Facts about Herman Cain's 9-9-9 Tax Plan, PolitiFact, September 26, 2011.

[7] Rachel O'Connor, Jeff Hayes, and Barbara Gault, *Paid Sick Days Access Varies by Race/ Ethnicity, Sexual Orientation, and Job Characteristics*, Institute for Women's Policy Research publication B337, July 2014.

[8] Bureau of Labor Statistics, Employee Benefits in the United States—March 2013, Table 6. Selected Paid Leave Benefits: Access, National Compensation Survey, March 2013; this and all other related statistics cited below refer only to workers outside the federal government.

[9] See, for example, the comments under the article Ranger Kidwell-Ross, WalMart Dissolves Relationship With USM throughout the United States, *Sweeping Industry News Bulletin*, April 1, 2011, retrieved September 30, 2014; many other quotes between $25 and $40 can be found on similar industry websites.

[10] Gilda Azurdia, Stephen Freedman, Gayle Hamilton, and Caroline Schultz, Encouraging Savings for Low- and Moderate-Income Individuals: Preliminary Implementation Findings from the SAVEUSA Evaluation, MDRC, 2013.

Chapter 11

[1] Bureau of Justice Statistics, *Correctional Populations in the United States, 2012*, publication NCJ 243936, December 2013.

[2] Calculations based on Organisation for Economic Co-Operation and Development, *OECD Factbook 2010: Economic, Environmental and Social Statistics*, Prison Population Rate, 2010.

[3] Roy Walmsley, *World Prison Population List*, 10th edition, International Centre for Prison Studies, 2013.

[4] The Sentencing Project, *Incarcerated Women*, September 2012.

[5] Bureau of Justice Statistics, *Prisoners in 2012*, publication NCJ243920, December 2013, Table 17, combined with population statistics from the Census Bureau's American FactFinder website.

[6] Bureau of Justice Statistics, *Prisoners in 2012*, publication NCJ243920, December 2013, Table 18.

[7] Maya Schenwar, *Locked Down, Locked Out: Why Prison Doesn't Work and How We Can Do Better*, Berrett-Koehler Publishers, page 74.

[8] Christy A. Visher , Sara A. Debus-Sherrill, and Jennifer Yahner, Employment After Prison: A Longitudinal Study of Former Prisoners, *Justice Quarterly*, 2011, 28:698-718, page 708.

[9] Sara Wakefield and Christopher Uggen, Incarceration and Stratification, *Annual Review of Sociology*, 2010, 36:387-406, page 388.

[10] Jeffrey Ian Ross et al, Knocking on the Ivory Tower's Door: The Experience of Ex-Convicts Applying for Tenure-Track University Positions, *Journal of Criminal Justice Education*, 2011, 22: 267-85.

[11] Scott Shane and Eric Lichtblau, Scientist Is Paid Millions by US in Anthrax Suit, *The New York Times*, June 28, 2008.

[12] European Commission, Factsheet on the "Right to Be Forgotten" Ruling, document C-131/12, June 3, 2014.

[13] Rania Khalek, How Private Prisons Game the System, Salon, December 2, 2011.

[14] David Shapiro, Banking on Bondage: Private Prisons and Mass Incarceration, ACLU, November 2, 2011, page 5.

NOTES

[15] Paul Ashton and Amanda Petteruti, Gaming the System: How the Political Strategies of Private Prison Companies Promote Ineffective Incarceration Strategies, Justice Policy Institute, June, 2011.

[16] Bureau of Justice Statistics, *Prisoners in 2012*, publication NCJ243920, December 2013, Appendix Table 7.

[17] Bureau of Justice Statistics, *Correctional Populations in the United States*, 2012, publication NCJ 243936, December 2013, page 1.

[18] Bureau of Justice Statistics, *Prisoners in 2012*, publication NCJ243920, December 2013, Table 1.

[19] Bureau of Justice Statistics, *Prisoners in 2012*, publication NCJ243920, December 2013, Table 4.

[20] Bureau of Justice Statistics, *Capital Punishment*, 2011 -- Statistical Tables, publication NCJ 242185, July 2013, Table 14.

[21] Bureau of Justice Statistics, *Capital Punishment*, 2011 -- Statistical Tables, publication NCJ 242185, July 2013, Table 17.

[22] Death Penalty Information Center, Executions by Year since 1976; there were 43 executions in 2012 and 38 in 2013.

[23] Centers for Disease Control and Prevention, FastStats: Assault or Homicide, retrieved September 30, 2014

[24] National Employment Law Project, 65 Million "Need not Apply": The Case for Reforming Criminal Background Checks for Employment, March 2011.

Chapter 12

[1] Justia US Law, Abortion,retrieved October 30, 2014.

[2] Jon O. Shimabukuro, *Abortion: Judicial History and Legislative Response*, Congressional Research Service report RL33467, March 24, 2014.

[3] Guttmacher Institute, *State Policies in Brief: An Overview of Abortion Laws*, October 1, 2014.

[4] Laura Basset, Anti-Abortion Laws Take Dramatic Toll On Clinics Nationwide, Huffington Post, August 26, 2013 (updated November 11, 2013).

[5] Guttmacher Institute, *State Policies in Brief: Targeted Regulation of Abortion Providers*, June 1, 2014.

[6] Aaron Winter, *Anti-Abortion Extremism and Violence in the United States, Extremism in America* (edited by George Michael), University Press of Florida, Gainesville, Florida, 2014, pages 218-248.

[7] Joe Stumpe and Monica Davey, Abortion Doctor Shot to Death in Kansas Church, *New York Times*, May 31, 2009.

[8] Operation Rescue, You Can Help Put George Tiller In Prison!, retrieved September 30, 2014.

[9] Operation Rescue, Death Throes of the Death Industry: A Record 87 Surgical Abortion Clinics Close in 2013, December 23, 2013.

[10] Gallup, Gallup Historical Trends: Abortion, accessed September 30, 2014, 2012-2014 average.

Chapter 13

[1] Brennan Center for Justice, States With New Voting Restrictions Since 2010 Election, June 18, 2014.

[2] Brennan Center for Justice, Citizens without Proof: A Survey of American's Possession of Documentary Proof of Citizenship and Photo Identification, November 2006.

[3] Project Vote, The Role of Challengers in Elections, January 3, 2008, page 4.

[4] Keith G. Bentele and Erin E. O'Brien, Jim Crow 2.0? Why States Consider and Adopt Restrictive Voter Access Policies, *Perspectives on Politics*, December, 2013: 1103.

[5] Charles Stewart III, Waiting to Vote in 2012, *Journal of Law and Politics*, 2013, 28:439-63, esp. page 458.

[6] Myrna Pérez, *Voter Purges*, Brennan Center for Justice, 2008, page 3.

[7] US Commission on Civil Rights, Voting Irregularities in Florida During the 2000 Presidential Election, June 2011, executive summary.

[8] Steve Freeman and Joel Bleifuss, *Was the 2004 Presidential Election Stolen? Exit Polls, Election Fraud, and the Official Count*, Seven Stories Press, New York, 2006.

[9] Adam Cohen, No One Should Have to Stand in Line for 10 Hours to Vote, *New York Times*, August 26, 2008.

[10] People for the American Way, NAACP, and Lawyers' Committee for Civil Rights under Law, Shattering the Myth: An Initial Snapshot of Voter Disenfranchisement in the 2004 Elections, December 2004

[11] United States Election Assistance Commission, A Summary of the 2004 Election Day Survey, September 2005, pages 1-2.

[12] Kathy Dopp et al, Analysis of the 2004 Presidential Election Exit Poll Discrepancies, USCountVotes, April 12, 2005, page 22.

[13] Robert F. Kennedy, Jr., Was the 2004 Election Stolen? *Rolling Stone*, June 15, 2006.

[14] Governors Highway Safety Association, Speed and Red Light Camera Laws, September 2014.

Chapter 14

[1] President Barack Obama, Press Conference by the President, August 1, 2014.

[2] President George W. Bush, Interview of the President by Yonit Levi, Channel 2 News, January 4, 2008.

[3] Office of the Assistant Attorney General, Memorandum for Alberto R Gonzales, Counsel to the President, August 1, 2002, page 1.

[4] Brian Ross and Richard Esposito, CIA's Harsh Interrogation Techniques Described, ABC News, November 18, 2005; Ewen MacAskill, Torture Techniques Endorsed by the Bush Administration, *Guardian*, April 18. 2009.

[5] US Army Field Manual 34-52 Intelligence Interrogation, pages 1-8; US Army Field Manual 2-22.3 Human Intelligence Collector Operations, September 6, 2006, pages 5-21.

[6] Craig Whitlock, Renditions Continue under Obama, Despite Due-Process Concerns, *Washington Post*, January 1, 2013.

[7] Cora Currier and Suevon Lee, The Best Reporting on Detention and Rendition Under Obama, ProPublica, July 13, 2012.

[8] Greg Miller, Plan for Hunting Terrorists Signals US Intends to Keep Adding Names to Kill Lists, *Washington Post*, October 23, 2012.

[9] Adam Entous, Special Report: How the White House Learned to Love the Drone, Reuters, May 18, 2010.

NOTES

[10] The Bureau of Investigative Journalism, Get the Data: Drone Wars, June 11, 2014.

[11] Continued Support for US Drone Strikes, Pew Research Center for the People & the Press, February 11, 2013; Bruce Drake, Report Questions Drone Use, Widely Unpopular Globally, but not in the US, Pew Research Center, October 23, 2013.

[12] Global Opposition to US Surveillance and Drones, but Limited Harm to America's Image, Pew Research Global Attitudes Project, July 14, 2014.

[13] Global Opinion of Barack Obama, Pew Research Global Attitudes Project, July 18, 2013.

[14] Public Sees US Power Declining as Support for Global Engagement Slips, Pew Research Center for the People & the Press, December 3, 2013.

[15] National Archives, Executive Order 12333—United States Intelligence Activities, Federal Register, December 4, 1981, section 1.12(b)(1).

[16] National Security Agency, Signals Intelligence, accessed September 21, 2014.

[17] President Barack Obama, Remarks by the President on Review of Signals Intelligence, January 17, 2014.

[18] Barton Gellman and Greg Miller, 'Black Budget' Summary Details US Spy Network's Successes, Failures and Objectives, *Washington Post*, August 29, 2013.

[19] James Bamford, The NSA Is Building the Country's Biggest Spy Center (Watch What You Say), *Wired*, March 15, 2012.

[20] Siobhan Gorman, Meltdowns Hobble NSA Data Center, *Wall Street Journal*, October 7, 2003; Kashmir Hill, NSA's Utah Data Center Suffers New Round Of Electrical Problems, *Forbes*, October 17, 2013.

[21] Jo Becker and Scott Shane, Secret 'Kill List' Proves a Test of Obama's Principles and Will, *New York Times*, May 29, 2012.

Chapter 15

[1] Lyrics by Clare Herbert Woolston (1856-1927).

[2] US Customs and Border Protection, Southwest Border Unaccompanied Alien Children, October 1, 2013 - August 31, 2014, Accessed September 30, 2014.

[3] Public Religion Research Institute, Nearly 7-in-10 Americans See Unaccompanied Children at Border as Refugees, Not Illegal Immigrants, July 29, 2014.

[4] United Nations High Commissioner for Refugees, About Refugees, quoting the 1951 Refugee Convention Relating to the Status of Refugees and associated protocols, accessed September 30, 2014.

[5] Cynthia J. Arnson and Eric L. Olson (eds.), *Organized Crime in Central America: The Northern Triangle*, Woodrow Wilson International Center for Scholars, November 2011.

[6] United Nations High Commissioner for Refugees Regional Office for the United States and the Caribbean, Children on the Run: Unaccompanied Children Leaving Central America and Mexico and the Need for International Protection, 2014.

[7] Jessica Jones and Jennifer Podkul, *Forced From Home: The Lost Boys and Girls of Central America*, Women's Refugee Commission, 2012, pages 10-11.

[8] United Nations High Commissioner for Refugees Regional Office for the United States and the Caribbean, Children on the Run: Unaccompanied Children Leaving Central America and Mexico and the Need for International Protection, 2014, page 34, New York.

[9] United States Conference of Catholic Bishops, Mission to Central America: The Flight of Unaccompanied Children to the United States, November, 2013, page 11.

[10] US Citizenship and Immigration Services, Refugees, November 4, 2013.

[11]   Brianna Lee, Why Aren't Central Americans Getting Asylum In The US? *International Business Times*, August 8, 2014; American Immigration Council Immigration Policy Center, *Mexican and Central American Asylum and Credible Fear Claims: Background and Context*, May 21, 2014, page 13.

[12]   United Nations High Commissioner for Refugees, Syrian Refugees: Inter-Agency Regional Update, September 18, 2014; figures for Turkey also include more than 150,000 migrants from Islamic State persecution in the last two weeks of September, 2014.

[13]   Michael Martinez and Holly Yan, Showdown: California Town Turns Away Buses of Detained Immigrants, CNN, July 3, 2014.

[14]   Public Religion Research Institute, Nearly 7-in-10 Americans See Unaccompanied Children at Border as Refugees, Not Illegal Immigrants, July 29, 2014.

[15]   Diana Villiers Negroponte, The Surge in Unaccompanied Children from Central America: A Humanitarian Crisis at Our Border, Brookings Up Front, July 2, 2014.

Chapter 16

[1]   Spencer Weart, The Modern Temperature Trend, American Institute of Physics, February 2014.

[2]   Myles R. Allen et al, Warming Caused by Cumulative Carbon Emissions towards the Trillionth Tonne, *Nature*, 2008, 458:1163-66.

[3]   Intergovernmental Panel on Climate Change, Climate Change 2014: Impacts, Adaptation, and Vulnerability, March 30, 2014.

[4]   Spencer Weart, The Carbon Dioxide Greenhouse Effect, American Institute of Physics, February 2014.

[5]   Pew Research Center, Climate Change: Key Data Points from Pew Research, January 27, 2014.

[6]   Carolina Martinez, Titan's Surface Organics Surpass Oil Reserves on Earth, NASA Cassini Mission, February 13, 2008.

[7]   Oil Shale and Tar Sands Programmatic Environmental Impact Statement Information Center, What Are Tar Sands? US Argonne National Laboratory, accessed September 30, 2014.

[8]   Alberta Energy, Alberta's Oil Sands: The Facts, January 2014.

[9]   M.L. Harris, *Guideline for Wetland Establishment on Reclaimed Oil Sands Leases* (2nd edition), Alberta Environment, 2008, page 81, Edmonton, Alberta.

[10]   NASA Earth Observatory, Athabasca Oil Sands, accessed September 30, 2014.

[11]   M.L. Harris, *Guideline for Wetland Establishment on Reclaimed Oil Sands Leases* (2nd edition), Alberta Environment, 2008, page 81, Edmonton, Alberta; Alberta Government, *Alberta Wetland Policy*, September, 2013, page 21.

[12]   Damian Carrington, Tar Sands Exploitation Would Mean Game Over for Climate, Warns Leading Scientist, *Guardian*, May 20, 2013.

[13]   US Environmental Protection Agency, Deepwater Horizon—BP Gulf of Mexico Oil Spill, retrieved September 30, 2014.

[14]   IHS, Weekly Rig Count, September 26, 2014.

[15]   Simon Goodley, Shell Presses Ahead with World's Deepest Offshore Oil Well, *Guardian*, May 9, 2013.

[16]   Andrew Callus, Offshore Oil Rigs Deeper than Ever, *Globe and Mail*, August 14, 2012.

[17]   Emily Schmall and Justin Juozapavicius, Answers on Link between Injection Wells and Quakes, Associated Press, July 14, 2014.

NOTES

[18] Michael Shellenberger, Ted Nordhaus, Alex Trembath, and Jesse Jenkins, *Where the Shale Gas Revolution Came From*, The Breakthrough Institute, May 2012, Oakland, California.

[19] Environmental Protection Agency, Regulation of Hydraulic Fracturing Under the Safe Drinking Water Act, Retrieved September 30, 2014.

[20] Lauren Pagel and Lisa Sumi, Loopholes for Polluters—The Oil and Gas Industry's Exemptions to Major Environmental Laws, Earthworks Oil & Gas Accountability Project, May 16, 2011.

[21] Energy Information Administration, Marcellus Region Production Continues Growth, August 5, 2014.

[22] Naveena Sadasivam, New York State of Fracking: A ProPublica Explainer, ProPublica, July 22, 2014.

[23] Energy Information Administration, *Technically Recoverable Shale Oil and Shale Gas Resources: An Assessment of 137 Shale Formations in 41 Countries Outside the United States*, June 2013, page 2, Washington, DC.

[24] Claudia Copeland, *Mountaintop Mining: Background on Current Controversies*, Congressional Research Service report RS21421, July 16, 2014.

[25] John McQuaid, Mining the Mountains, *Smithsonian Magazine,* January 2009.

[26] Environmental Protection Agency, *The Effects of Mountaintop Mines and Valley Fills on Aquatic Ecosystems of the Central Appalachian Coalfields*, 2011, page 2, Washington, DC.

[27] Environmental Protection Agency, *The Effects of Mountaintop Mines and Valley Fills on Aquatic Ecosystems of the Central Appalachian Coalfields*, 2011, page 10, Washington, DC.

[28] National Mining Association, *Mountaintop Mining Fact Book,* March 2009, pages 4-5, Washington, DC.

[29] Ross Geredien, Post-Mountaintop Removal Reclamation of Mountain Summits for Economic Development in Appalachia, Natural Resources Defense Council, December 7., 2009, page 3, Washington, DC.

[30] Richard K. Lattanzio, Canadian Oil Sands: Life-Cycle Assessments of Greenhouse Gas Emissions, Congressional Research Service report R42537, March 10, 2014, page 11.

[31] Donald L. Gautier et al, Circum-Arctic Resource Appraisal: Estimates of Undiscovered Oil and Gas North of the Arctic Circle, US Geological Survey, 2008.

[32] Jeff Tollefson, Air Sampling Reveals High Emissions from Gas Field, *Nature*, February 7, 2012.

Index

GOULD TRUST FUND
320.473
Babones
5-15   c2015

ABOUT THE AUTHOR

Photo courtesy of Aija Bruvere

Salvatore Babones is an associate professor in sociology and social policy at the University of Sydney in Australia and an associate fellow at the Institute for Policy Studies in Washington, DC. He holds both a master's degree in statistics and a Ph.D. in sociology from the Johns Hopkins University. He is the author or editor of ten books and has published more than two dozen academic journal articles in addition to numerous book chapters and other pieces. Before moving to Australia in 2008, he taught for five years at the University of Pittsburgh, where he was assistant professor of sociology, public health, and public and international affairs. Prior to becoming a full-time academic he worked in the private sector in financial risk management. His previous books *Social Inequality and Public Health* (2009) and *The Future of Development: A Radical Manifesto* (2013, co-authored with Gustavo Esteva and Philipp Babcicky) were published by Policy Press in cooperation with the University of Chicago Press.